The Nature and Character of Theology

An Introduction to the Thought of J. A. Quenstedt
from
THEOLOGIA DIDACTICO-POLEMICA SIVE
SYSTEMA THEOLOGICUM

Abridged, edited, and translated by
Luther Poellot

Publishing House
St. Louis

Library of Congress Cataloging-in-Publication Data

Quenstedt, Johann Andreas, 1617-1688.
        The nature and charcter of theology.

        Translation of the first three chapters of: Theologia didactico-polemica
sive systema theologicum.
        1. Lutheran Church—Doctrines—Early works to 1800. 2. Theology, Doc-
trinal—Early works to 1800. I. Poellot Luther. II. Title.
BX8064.Q462513 1986   230'.41   85-17068
ISBN 0-570-03984-3 (pbk.)

---

1 2 3 4 5 6 7 8 9 10   WVI   95 94 93 92 91 90 89 88 87 86

Contents

Contents

Translator's Foreword

Quenstedt's *Theologia didactico-polemica sive systema theologicum,* one of the most massive volumes in Lutheran literature, consists of 4 parts, 48 chapters, 2,073 large pages in the 1696 edition (used for this translation), and 3 indexes. A former owner of the present translator's copy noted that it weighs 11 pounds and 2 ounces.

This translation of the first three chapters (53 pages in the Latin) is abridged only by omission of detailed references to sources, many of which are not readily available; those who feel a need to search further will find the Latin Quenstedt, and perhaps some sources used for it, in libraries that have such materials. Other editorial efforts involved mainly correction of typographical errors and addition of notes.

As for Bible quotations, no one English version was used in this work, largely because it was common in the 17th century to cite Scripture freely according to sense, rather than verbatim (the latter usually only when necessary to make a specific point); as a result, Quenstedt and his sources generally speak for themselves, in a sense and so far as possible, also in these passages.

The undersigned offers this small part of a large classic in the hope that it will find charity among critics and that some day perhaps the entire work will be properly Englished.

Preface

Johann Quenstedt ranks after Martin Chemnitz (1522–86) and Johann Gerhard (1582–1637) as probably the most influential Lutheran leader in the post-Reformation era. As professor at the university at Wittenberg he was the real leader of Lutheran orthodoxy, of which his *Theologia* is certainly a standard. His times cannot be fully understood without knowledge of it, and our times can only profit by knowledge of it.

Johann(es) Andreas Quenstedt (Aug. 13, 1617—May 22, 1688) was born in Quedlinburg (now in East Germany), 33 miles SW of Magdeburg and 12 miles SE of Halberstadt. His was an old and respected family tree. His father, Ludolf Quenstedt, was a partrician and a canon (or prebendary) of St. Mary Church, Halberstadt. His mother, nee Dorothea Gerhard, was a sister of Johann Gerhard.

Until he was 16, Quenstedt received private education, first at home and then in the home of Friedrich Lentz, doctor of law and chancellor at Quedlinburg. From 16 to 20 he attended public school.

His hope and plan to begin studying theology in 1637 at Jena under his uncle, Johann Gerhard, was thwarted by the latter's death. His mother then, albeit with some misgiving about the doctrinal stance of the university at Helmstedt (founded 1576 by Julius, duke of Brunswick), sent her son there, because it was close to home (about 50 miles NW of Quedlinburg).

After six years at Helmstedt, Quenstedt spent about nine months at home and then, in 1644, went to the university at Wittenberg, where he continued his studies. As early as Oct. 19, 1644, he established himself as a university lecturer. He lectured on geography; became adjunct professor in the philosophical faculty 1646, while continuing his study of theology; was full professor of logic and metaphysics and associate professor of theology 1649–60, and full professor of theology 1660–88.

Quenstedt became a widower twice without children and married again in 1656. A daughter of this union became the wife of 72-year-old Abraham Calov in 1684.

Our times—like those of Quenstedt—bear the mark of religious tension and controversy. They call for clear vision of the issues involved, solid grounding in the Word of God, and an approach that bears promise and kindles hope and faith.

Because of his association with Helmstedt, Quenstedt at first met a cool reception engendered by wariness and distrust when he went to Wittenberg, a base of Lutheran orthodoxy. But Prof. Wilhelm Leyser (1592–1649; son of Polykarp Leyser the Elder [1552–1610]) provided him with room and board, and under his influence and that of Prof. Johann Hülsemann (1602–61) he was won for Lutheran orthodoxy. So he held the views set forth as his in his *Theologia* out of conviction based on experience and personal study—and not, as some might think, because he was, so to say, born and bred that way.

In his approach to inter-Lutheran, Lutheran-Reformed, and Lutheran-Catholic tensions, Quenstedt was not a fiery protagonist but was mild, retiring, and unpretentious. He let his adversaries, as well as those who sided with him, speak for themselves and included quotations from them in his work. He built his *Theologia* on the pattern of *Theologia positivo-acroamatica* by Johann Friedrich König (1619–64)—and freely added his own independent judgment. It is therefore not accurate to dismiss him as the "bookkeeper and secretary" of Wittenberg Lutheran orthodoxy (the phrase is that of Friedrich August Tholuck [1799–1877], an opponent of Lutheran orthodoxy).

Rather, "to be able to pass a proper judgment on Quenstedt, one must have read him and compared him with other dogmaticians" (F. Pieper, *Christian Dogmatics;* German, I, 175, note 582; English, I, 151, note 204). One reason for this book is to provide an opportunity to read him.

His gentle and irenic but firm approach to doctrinal problems is a model for our times. Even as Polykarp Leyser had counseled against hanging gratuitous tags and nicknames in adverse reflection on others, so Quenstedt's use of the term "Novators," for example, for the Helmstedt theologians is not name-calling but accurate shorthand for what was going on there.

His *Theologia* is nothing if not systematic. Each chapter is divided into two parts, didactic and polemic, the latter not being a hot war but a cool, calm, collected, and considered answer—a Lutheran reply, if you will—to questions, mind-sets, and theological stances that attacked or threatened to attack doctrine, faith, and practice based on the Word. What a handy tool! Doctrinal problems that confront us today are really not completely new. Some of the concerns of the times on which Quenstedt focuses—from the times of Leonhard Hutter (1553–1616) to those of Abraham Calov (1612–86)—are concerns of our times, for example: the need to respect the authority of the Word of God, to distinguish between moral philosophy and theology, and to recognize religious syncretism as a misguided attempt at union without unity.

Quenstedt's *Theologia* was not a one-time shot in the dark of theologically unsettled times. After it first appeared in 1685, it was reissued at least five times: 1691, 1696, 1701, 1702, and 1717. Yet as a result of neglect, when Latin fell into disuse, it was, as far as the present writer has been able to determine, not translated except in scattered fragments. The present book, then, which covers only chapters 1–3 of Part I, may be the first to present any part of the work in a separate volume in English.

Consider also this: Johann Sebastian Bach (1685–1750) was 3 when Quenstedt died. And as Bach grew up and gave the world his music, under the strong influence of Lutheranism, Quenstedt's work helped to make his world of song what it was and is, insofar as it can be said to soar on the wings of his Lutheran faith.

Finally, why specifically this selection from Quenstedt's *Theologia?*

If one is to begin at all, one must begin somewhere. The most logical place is at the beginning—which is where this book begins.

The beginning, in this case, goes to the very foundation of anything that may be properly called theology in the basic sense of the word. It is a point of orientation for all that follows. For lack of reliable orientation, much religion today is adrift. Theology is thought of by many as the sum of man's thinking about God (or about some kind of a god or gods), and as such it is conceived of as originating with man and somehow reaching upward. Quenstedt begins with the word *theology,* clears the air as to what it means, shows how true theology does not originate with man but is given to man by God—not a god of man's imagination and creation, but specifically the Triune God (discussed at much greater length later in *Theologia*)—and leads you into the Word (e.g., in Thesis IV of the didactic part of Chapter 1: "We prove this thesis from Matt. 11:27").

That is also the prime purpose of this book: not so much to lead you into Quenstedt, as with his help to lead you into the Word.

Luther Poellot

Chapter I
Of Theology in General

Section I

Didactic

Thesis I

Theology, if you consider the force and use of the word, is nothing else than the teaching about God and divine things, as pneumatology is the teaching or doctrine about spirits and astrology is the teaching about stars.

Note I. Two things are to be observed here: 1. The notation of the name; 2. the notation of the things designated by the name. The notation of the name is handled[1] by a statement of its (1) origin, (2) meaning, and (3) use.

Note II. As to origin, the name "theology" is not simple but is composed of the words *theos* and *logos*. But one must distinguish here between the *logos tou theou* [Word of God] and the *logos peri tou theou* [word (or teaching) about God]. The Word of God, or, as we have it in Ro 3:2 and Heb 5:12, *ta logia tou theou* [the oracles of God], is Holy Scripture itself, the source[2] of theology. But *logos peri tou theou* [word (or teaching) about God] is theology, authoritative teaching[3] about Him.[4]

Note III. Some Calvinists, for example Antonius Walaeus, Johann Scharp, and Ludwig Crocius, say that the word *theologia* properly means *logos tou theou*, Word of God[5] or what God says.[6] But we prove our view (1) from the nature of the concrete and of the abstract. The concrete, "theologian," and the abstract, "theology," derive[7] from one primary form. However, a theologian is not God speaking, but is one who speaks about God. So also is theology not the Word of God, but is the word about God.[8] (2) From the derivation of the word. The derivation of the word "theology" is to be made from the verb *theologein*, that is, to speak about God, to proclaim[9] God. (3) From the analogy of similar words. So pneumatology is not the word[10] [or teaching] or discourse of the Spirit, but the teaching about spirits. Astrology is not what stars teach,[11] but the teaching about stars. So theology is not the word of God Himself, but the teaching[12] about God. (4) From the difference between Holy Scripture and theology. Scripture is the source of theology, that is, *logos tou theou* [the Word of God]; theology is the authoritative teaching and *logos peri tou theou* [doctrine about God].

Note IV. Theology is rightly named after God, for (1) it is originally from God, (2) it deals as to its subject[13] with God, (3) as to its end, it goes[14] to God, and (4) as to its effect, it leads a person to God. Hence Thomas[15] [says]: "Theology is taught by God, teaches God, and leads to God." And thus theology properly takes its name from God. For if you consider the principal efficient cause, God is its author, with mediating revelation made through the Word; or [if you consider] the object, or subject matter,[16] it is God; or finally, [if you consider] the end[17] itself, God is the end thereof and that salutary and glorious vision of God, toward which we strive, led by this knowledge of God. But the thrust itself of the name is taken not so much from the efficient principle[18] or from the end as from the subject[19] of [or under] consideration, so that it is *logos peri theou*, the doctrine[20] about God.

Note V. In the composition of this word, the name *theos* [God] denotes not only God Himself, One in essence, Three in persons, but at the same time there are included *ta tou theou*, [the things] that are God's, or divine things. For theology is concerned with God, both *in casu recto* [in the nominative case] and *obliquo* [oblique (here genitive) case], as the scholastics say, that is, with God Himself and the things that are God's.

Note VI. Distinguish between the adequate[21] and the inadequate[22] subject of theology. The inadequate and primary is God, One in essence, Three in persons. The adequate is all divine things, or God Himself and whatever is God's and whatever is from God and is directed[23] to God. And so the word "God" is either to be extended, so that it includes also the things that are God's, or one must add that theology is the doctrine about God and about divine things.

Note VII. As to the meaning of the name "theology," one must distinguish between (1) its most general meaning, which denotes any teaching[24] or doctrine about God, either true or false, especially in profane authors; (2) [its] general [meaning], which designates any kind of knowledge of God whatever, yet true, also natural; (3) [its] special [meaning], which denotes the knowledge of God and of divine mysteries revealed and taught in the Scriptures; and (4) [its] most special [meaning], which designates the part of heavenly doctrine that deals with Christ's deity, so that it is the teaching *peri logou tou theou*, about the hypostatic Word of God, in which sense among the fathers *theologein ton logon* is to assert the divinity of Christ, and John the apostle and evangelist, the singular forerunner of this mystery, is called theologian in the inscription of the Apocalypse. He is called theologian evangelist by the Damascene,[25] namely because he clearly and notably expressed *theoteeta tou logou* [the divinity of the Word], with the other evangelists occupied with *oikonomia* [economy], that is, the doctrine of the incarnation of the Son of God and the restoration of mankind that was wrought thereby.

Note VIII. As to the use of the name "theology," one must observe that the word "theology" was first used by

Gentiles, for very ancient Greek writers, as Lactantius says, are called theologians because they deal with gods and their worship, and their knowledge [is called] theology; and thereafter that word was also used by Christians.

Note IX. Distinguish between the word "theology" taken in the abstract (and so it is *agraphos* [unwritten] as to writing, for it is not found in Holy Scripture) and the word "theology" taken in the concrete (and in this way it is *eggraphos* [inscribed]). For we have it in the inscription of the Apocalypse, in which the evangelist John is called the chief theologian, *kat' exocheen ho theologos*. And though some object that this title is not found in all Greek copies, nor in the Syriac version, yet most of the more correct codices have it, so that most hold it as added by John himself, not for the sake of glorying but [by reason] of the truth.

Note X. Though the name "theology" in the abstract is not found in Scripture as regards the sound, yet we have it there as regards the sense, since it uses various synonyms *isodynama* [of the same force as that] of that name. For it is called simply[26] wisdom, 1 Co 2:6, and, with an addition, wisdom of God, v. 7; word of wisdom, 1 Co 12:8; manifold wisdom, Eph 3:10; knowledge of salvation, Lk 1:77; full knowledge of the truth which [truth] is according to godliness, Tts 1:1; exposition of the way of God, Acts 18:26; form, or pattern, of sound words, 2 Ti 1:13; the doctrine that is according to godliness, 1 Ti 6:3; teaching by God, 1 Th 4:9; mind of the Spirit, Ro 8:6.

Thesis II

The name "theology" has a twofold homonym, or like-sounding and like-spelled word,[27] one pure, the other analogic. The pure homonym is when the name "theology" is used also of theology that is false and subject to opinion, for example of mythology, of Jewish and Turkish falsehoods, of heretical idle talk, of teratology, or strange scholastic and all [other] kinds of theology, etc.

Note I. Dividing theology into true and false is only nominal and entirely and purely equivocal. For false theology, which is also called subject to opinion,[28] shares nothing but the name "theology" and is only wrongly so called, since, on the basis of 1 Ti 4:2 and Tts 1:10 it should rather be called idle talk and lies and is no more theology than a picture of a horse is a horse.

Note II. In Scripture, false theology is called doctrine of devils, 1 Ti 4:1, and devilish wisdom, Ja 3:15, because it has the devil, the father of falsehood, Jn 8:44, as source, and it is nothing else than a false opinion and contrary to the heavenly truth about God and His will and works.

Note III. Distinguish between original false theology and that which was begun or was originated. The original is in the devil himself and can be called wickedness without a teacher, Jn 8:44: "When he speaks a lie, he speaks from his own nature."[29] For he himself is *tees kakias heuretees* [the inventor of wickedness], as Methodius calls him, "the source and inventor of wickedness [and] the craftsman and inventor of heresy and sin." It was begun or scattered about in mankind among people misled by the devil, and it deals either with fictitious gods (or gods falsely so called), as heathen theology or [that] of the Gentiles, or it teaches falsely about the true God, as the theology of the Jews, Samaritans, Turks, heretics, and false Christians, etc.

Note IV. The form of heathen theology, or that of the Gentiles, consists (1) in *polytheia*, or the fiction of many gods and the worship and adoration of creatures and

demons under statues and idols; (2) in turpitude and
filthiness of morals and life; and it is not so much
theology or knowledge of God as ignorance of the true
God, G1 4:8, and Godlessness, Eph 2:12.

Note V. The source[30] of heathen theology as such is
the oracles and responses of demons, the auguries of
soothsayers, the presentiments of dreams, and the
divinations of magi.

Note VI. The Jewish or Talmudic falsehood is that
which, rejecting the books of the New Testament, accepts
only the Old Testament, but corrupts it by Talmudic
traditions and rabbinical fabrications, perverts the sense of
many statements of Scripture, rejects and with horrible
blasphemies execrates the true Messiah and Redeemer of
the world—who was manifested in the flesh long ago
already—and looks for another to come. In a word, the
theology of the Talmudists and rabbis does not heal but
sickens, for (1) it adulterates and perverts statements of
the Bible; (2) it contains express blasphemy; and (3) it
peddles endless Aesopic mataeology [idle talk], etc.[31]

Note VII. The source and norm of Judaic theology
and religion is the Talmud (Hebrew *Talmud,* so to say[32]
body of doctrine,[33] from the root *lamad,* he learned, in
Piel *limmed,* he made to learn, he taught), or the
doctrinal book of the Jews, containing all their divine and
human knowledge, compiled from the views of many
rabbis and filled with many and various fables and
corruptions of the Scriptures. Its two parts are the
Mishnah, that is, secondary[34] and oral law or text, and
the Gemara, or explanation. And the Talmud is twofold:
that of Jerusalem, which was compiled at Tiberias in the
third century after the birth of Christ, and the
Babylonian, which began in the fourth century; and the
latter outranked the former in its esteem. "Differences
between the Jerusalem and the Babylonian Mishnah are
endless in words and extremely many in substance," says
John Lightfoot.

Note VIII. Samaritan theology was neither altogether

Israelite nor altogether heathen, but as it were a kind of monstrosity compacted from a variety admixture of religions. For the Samaritans worshiped the true God and the false gods of the Gentiles equally, mixed Jewish ceremonies with superstitions of the Gentiles, 2 K 17:32 ff., [and] accepted only the Pentateuch or only the Five Books of Moses, rejecting all the rest, historical as well as prophetic [books]; some understand this only of rejection from reading in synagogues.

Note IX. The Muhammadan or Turkish mataeology acknowledges as author the pseudoprophet and impostor Muhammad, who, by spread of detestable teaching, began to gather followers in the seventh century after the birth of Christ. Its norm and source is the Koran (which they allow none but Muhammadans to touch, and those clean and washed; hence they inscribed on its container these words: "Let no one but one who is clean touch it"), a book filled up with absurdities and nonsense [and] put together from the Talmudic books of the Jews, Muhammadan falsehoods, and dreams of heretics like Arians, Nestorians, Manichaeans, and also of Epicureans, etc.

Note X. Pseudo-Christian theology is a mark of those who above all impugn the article of the most holy Trinity in one divine Essence of persons, the foundation of Christianity, and Baptism as its door, deny and, as much as in them lies, overturn the merit and satisfaction of Christ and yet hide under the shield of the name Christian, for example the Socinians, Anabaptists, [and] Shakers or Quakers in England.

Note XI. The heretical mataeology is that which either directly and expressly or by appealing[85] and close[86] reasoning denies and impugns one or more articles of faith that must be believed for salvation and defends and contends for other, unwholesome, pernicious, and deadly teachings, as Augustine says. And so heresy is error [that is] contrary to truth divinely revealed and that overturns the foundation of salvation.

Note XII. Teratology, or the unusual and obscure scholastic theology, which [was] born at Lutetia Parisiorum,[37] with Lombard as father, and [was] brought out at the Sorbonne, [and] finally spread and scattered through every Western church in the 13th century after the birth of the Savior, is nothing else, as Erasmus holds in *The Praise of Folly*, than "a discipline assembled by a kind of mixture from divine oracles and philosophical arguments like the Minotaur from a race of centaurs," or as blessed[88] Luther calls it in the book against Latomus, "ignorance of the truth and vain falsehood." For in the *Summas* the scholastics brought to the mysteries of faith their own conclusions from logical, physical, and metaphysical principles, disregarding or touching with a light hand the statements of Scripture. Hence Henry Cornelius Agrippa expressly says in the preface of [his] book on the vanity of sciences: "Scholastics try to prove and confirm the law of Christ by teachings of philosophers and ascribe more to them than to the holy prophets, evangelists, and apostles of God." Moreover they raise and defend idle, ridiculous, curious, useless, vain, [and] profane superstitions [and] sometimes also wicked and blasphemous questions. Doubtful matters, which move endlessly[39] around the highest articles of faith, are mostly of this kind, that they are more learnedly not known than known. Gisbert Voet makes scholastic theology consist of four parts: textual, or scripturary[40] (which he calls "poor, corrupt, imperfect, [and] uncommon[41]"), dogmatic-questionary, canonistic, and (which is put together from all those) summistic or casuistic. Dorsche says: "Scholastic theology is the mother of many strange fancies."

Note XIII. Syncretistic theology is a combination of religions and cults or a commixture of different religions—the product of the nature of carnal, inopportune zeal for peace—decreeing that fraternal—and that spiritual—fellowship in Christ be established and cultivated with papists and Calvinists, even if they still retain, defend, and contend for their errors and reject, oppose, and attack heavenly truth. Syncretism, which is the soul of Arminianism, posits in place of a foundation that dissent does not concern a foundation of faith, and thus Reformed and papists can be tolerated without harm to faith and salvation.

Note XIV. Skeptic or doubting theology is the theology of the neutrals, or freethinkers, who determine nothing [and] establish nothing, believe now nothing now everything, [and] embrace now this now that, according to the nature of the occasion or of the need. This theology is also called Placentine, versatile, mundane, political, opportunist,[42] horary, also doubtful or rather cothurnate. The Calvinists of Holland[43] ascribe this doubting theology—to be ascribed also to quodlibetarian scholastics—to Arminians.

Thesis III

According to the homonym that we have called analogic,[44] true theology is divided into archetypal or prototypal, that is, original-model [theology], and ectypal,[45] or expressed and fashioned [theology]. Archetypal theology is essentially in God, and it is that very same infinite wisdom of God by which God knows Himself in Himself (for the omniscient God cannot in any way be ignorant of Himself) and outside of Himself all things through Himself by an indivisible and immutable act of knowledge. Ectypal theology is nothing else than a certain expressed or rather foreshadowed image and form of that infinite and essential theology, either shared in this world or to be communicated in that which is to come by God, graciously and out of pure goodness, with intelligent creatures, according to their ability.[46]

Note I. This distinction is not of a univocal in its one meaning, but of an analog in its counterpart.[47] For archetypal theology is in the first place called theology. For it is the uncreated, infinite wisdom of the essential nature of God existing in the divine mind itself. But ectypal theology is secondarily called theology, because [it is] fashioned by it and is formed out according to it as [to] a divine and immutable pattern, and it is secondary, created, [and] finite. Archetypal theology is the substance and, with regard to the thing, the very infinite essence of God. Ectypal [theology] is an aptitude[48] and is included in the genus of quality.

Note II. Archetypal theology is the origin and beginning of all wisdom, and ectypal [theology] is an outflowing and effulgence, a kind of emanation and relucence, or image, thereof. The former is untaught wisdom, wisdom without a teacher; the latter is the taught word of wisdom, the word of wisdom that is taught and learned, 1 Co 2:13. The former is completely perfect [and] whole and at the same time an altogether pure act; the latter is imperfect, partial, separate, of the nature of an ability.[49]

Thesis IV

Archetypal theology is not only in God but [is] also God Himself, who in this is marvelously that which is known, the One who knows, [and] knowledge. That is, He [is] the subject itself that knows, the object itself that is known, and the knowledge itself; or, the theological matter, the theologian, and theology. For to be [God], and to know [God], and to savor of God are the same thing. Since archetypal theology is essential to the divine nature, therefore, as the very essence of God, so also is this knowledge of God common to the Father, the Son, and the Holy Spirit.

We prove this thesis from Mt 11:27: "No one knows the Son but the Father; and no one knows the Father but the Son and he to whom the Son wills to reveal Him"; and 1 Co 2:10–11: "The Spirit (of God) searches all things, also the deep things of God; and no one but the Spirit of God knows the things that are of God."

Observe (1). Some translators hold that in the former passage *epiginooskein* [thoroughly knows] is put for *ginooskein* [knows]; but Chrysostom much more correctly wants accurate knowledge to be thus designated.

Observe (2). In the same passage the knowledge by which the divine persons intimately and most perfectly know one another is ascribed only to the Father and the Son; but that exclusive [particle] does not exclude the Holy Spirit but that which is different from the divine nature, that is, creatures, according to the theological axiom: "When the exclusive particles 'alone, solely, only,' and similar ones in divine things are added to essential attributes, they exclude only other essences and things of a different nature." And so that we might understand that the Holy Spirit is not excluded from this, the apostle in the latter passage claims for the Holy Spirit the search and knowledge of all things, which [search and knowledge] are God's. We therefore have these three [facts]: The things that are of God no one knows but the Father, no one knows but the Son, [and] no one knows but the Holy Spirit.

Observe (3). The word *ereunan* here does not denote laborious search but accurate knowledge; this is true only in divine things, for divine *ereuneesis* [search] takes place

by simple beholding, without any labor of search. In this
passage there is therefore ascribed to the Holy Spirit a
search not of one who doesn't know (as Crell[50] would
have it) but of the simple beholding of one who
penetrates and most accurately knows all things, as God
and Christ are elsewhere said to search the reins and
hearts, Ps 7:9; Jer 11:20; Ro 8:27; Rv 2:23; in fact, [He,]
of whom it is said 1 Co 2:10, "He searches," of Him it is
said in v. 11, "He knows," so that you might know that
in v. 10 that which precedes is put for that which
follows.

Thesis V

This divine and inscrutable archetypal
theology belongs to Christ the God-man (1) by
nature and essentially, insofar as He is God, (2)
on account of the union or personally, insofar as
He is man, or according to the human nature, in
which respect it is also called theology of the
union, since by virtue of the hypostatic union [of
His two natures in His person] it is communicated in time to the assumed soul[51] of Christ.

Note: Franciscus Junius and Alsted[52] say that
archetypal theology is incommunicable because, as the
Deity's own, it could not be shared with any created
thing; but it is communicative, not properly of its very
self but only of its image; and thence they further infer
that that essential theology cannot be communicated to
the human nature of Christ. But one must distinguish
between created things left to themselves or constituted
outside of God, and the human nature of Christ
subsisting in the hypostasis of the Son of God. We grant
that to the former only[58] the image of the infinite wisdom

of God can be transmitted; but we affirm that the infinite and essential wisdom of God itself is truly and really communicated to the humanity of Christ.

We prove our thesis from Cl 2:3: "In whom are hidden all the treasures of wisdom and knowledge."

Observe (1) that *en hoo* is not to be referred to the term "mystery," v. 2, so that the sense would be: "In the mystery of God and of Christ," that is, in the Gospel, "all the treasures of wisdom and knowledge are hidden," as Zanchi,[54] Pareus,[55] and other Calvinists would have it—but to the immediately preceding "Christ." For relative pronouns are ordinarily to be referred to the immediately antecedent, not to remote, nouns, unless the thrust of the context or[56] another weighty reason advises something else. And the subject here is not "mystery" or Gospel but the person of Christ, as is clear from a comparison with v. 9.

Observe (2). The discussion is not about riches of created and finite wisdom, as the Calvinists likewise contend, but of increate and infinite [wisdom]. For in Scripture the latter, not the former, is called by the name of all riches of wisdom and knowledge and is explained by way of synonymity by "the depth of the riches both of the wisdom and knowledge of God," Ro 11:33.

Observe (3). Though the text does not speak expressly about the humanity of Christ, but about Christ, as Wendelin[57] protests, it cannot be understood except of the human nature, since the riches of wisdom and knowledge cannot properly be hidden in the deity of Christ, since wisdom itself is essentially infinite. And thus all the riches of wisdom and knowledge are to be understood as hidden in Christ according to the nature according to which "the fullness of the Godhead" dwells in Him, Cl 2:9, that is, the human [nature]. And that the discussion here is about Christ as man, or according to the human nature, is manifestly clear from the word "hidden"; for those riches of wisdom and knowledge were indeed held in the humanity of Christ in the state of humiliation, yet

nevertheless they rarely appeared or were manifested; cf.
Ph 2:6-8.

Thesis VI

Ectypal theology, which we have said to be
finite and created, is various according to the
nature either of the subjects to which God
communicates it or of the mode of
communicating, which is either common or
individual. For one ectypal theology is given in
Christ, according to His human nature, another
in the angels, another in human beings.

Note I. Both archetypal and ectypal theology are
proper to the human nature of Christ; archetypal
[theology] belongs to Him personally and communicatively,
or by reason of the hypostatic communication, and
ectypal [theology] inheres in Him by way of nature[58] and
subjectively. And though ectypal theology or Christ's
inherent[59] knowledge is completely perfect, yet it is not
infinite but created and finite, nor does it properly and
precisely belong to the assumed human nature by power
of the hypostatic union, or, speaking accurately, it is a
result and effect of the personal union.

Note II. Brochmand[60] does ill count that immeasurable
knowledge of the Son of God that (Christ) obtained by
the personal union among the kinds of ectypal theology,
since it is that very same archetypal theology of God.
They also speak invalidly and less accurately who call the
inherent[61] theology of Christ the man "theology of
union," since properly that other, namely divine, infinite,
[and] communicated wisdom comes by that name, since
the soul of Christ rejoices in it through and because of
the personal union.

Thesis VII

The ectypal theology of the human nature of Christ is not only connate but also infused by inspiration of God and acquired by experience and intuitive by excellence. The former, namely inherent and experimental, belonged to Christ in the days of [His] flesh and inhered subjectively and formally in His humanity and allowed increase, Lk 2:40. The latter, namely intuitive, He now enjoys in the other life and it becomes Him in a far better and more eminent way than any heavenly or blessed ones, by virtue of the glorification of [His] human nature.

Note: The Calvinists wonderfully praise the ectypal theology of Christ the man and call it "quasi divine and close to divine, quasi infinite and close to infinite," in fact "infinite," but only[62] with regard to objects and our small knowledge, in order the better to maintain that that infinite and essential wisdom was not communicated by the Logos to the assumed flesh. To that end also they perversely wrest the statements of the fathers, with which they everywhere decry the infinite wisdom of the human nature of Christ, to the wisdom proper to the soul of Christ and the same inhering subjectively and formally [in it], whereas they themselves sufficiently explain themselves that they mean infinite and divine wisdom and from it fully prove also the essential deity of Christ against the Arians.

We prove this thesis from Lk 2:40: "And the child grew and was strengthened by the Spirit, full of wisdom; and the grace of God was in Him"; v. 52: "And Jesus grew in wisdom and age and in grace before God and men."

Observe (1). Increase of wisdom is here said regarding Christ not with regard to deity but humanity. For just as increase in age pertained to the humanity of Christ, not the divinity, so also increase of wisdom pertained to the same humanity, not divinity.

Observe (2). Also then, when the man Christ Jesus grew in (inherent)[63] wisdom, v. 52, He was "full of wisdom," v. 40. There was therefore one wisdom in Christ according to [His] human nature, of which [wisdom] He was immediately full from the first moment of [His] conception, namely divine and infinite, through and because of the hypostatic union (for "the whole fullness" as "of the Godhead" so also "of divine wisdom and knowledge" dwelt personally in the assumed flesh, Cl 2:3 and 9), and another, in which He could gradually grow and which allowed growth, namely human and finite wisdom.

Observe (3). Christ grew according to [His] humanity in experimental and inherent knowledge, not in effect of demonstration, nor as a teacher is said to grow by disciples that grow, nor finally according to the view and opinion of men, so that He did not so much grow as appeared to men to have grown, as Bellarmine would have it, but the Savior grew really and truly in Himself. For as the Savior grew in stature and age and in grace in Himself and in respect to Himself,[64] so He also truly grew both in wisdom in Himself and in respect to Himself, since growth of these three are equally asserted in Luke with one copulative axiom.

Observe (4). If it be granted that Christ grew in wisdom only according to the view and opinion of men, they have what the Manichaeans want, namely that the Son of God was also incarnate according to a view, and the Calvinists, that Christ suffered and died for the reprobate according to a view.

Thesis VIII

The theology of the good angels is both concreate, or natural by creation, and accessory, and that both intuitive, or of sight by [their] preservation and confirmation in bliss, as well as experimental or acquired, which is perfected partly by revelation, partly by discourse and reasoning.

Note: We have nothing to say[65] about the evil angels, because they have for the most part lost their concreate and natural wisdom. There neither was, nor is, nor will be intuitive theology or [theology] of sight in them. For they never will be admitted to the beatific vision of God, because that requires sinlessness or immunity from sinning. But we grant experimental and acquired theology to the devils. For the impure spirits know God in such a way that they fear and tremble, Jas 2:19, and [they know] most divine mysteries, as is clear from Mk 5:7; Mt 8:29; and other passages.

We prove this thesis (a) from Mt 18:10: "Their" (that is, the little ones') "angels in heaven always behold the face of My Father, who is in heaven."

Observe (1). The term "to see" is not said of any and every kind of cognition, but of clear, distinct [cognition] and which in the mind and spirit would correspond in a way to the sight of the eyes, by which they discern physical and colored things.

Observe (2). "To see the face of God" does not denote precisely "to await God's command," as Arminius would have it (though it connotes [that]), but the beatific vision of God. Therefore the angels clearly and directly look upon the divine essence. But comprehensive and full vision of God does not belong to angels, assuredly finite spirits.

Observe (3). "Always" to see the face of the Father is never not to be present before God and to behold the face of the heavenly Father, which is His divine essence, glory, and majesty, without end.

Observe (4). The angels are in heaven and heavenly angels also when they are engaged in guarding children on earth. For they are established [and] confirmed in heaven, and also in the midst of guarding children they always behold the face of the heavenly Father, for that is demanded by the added statement "always" and the force of Christ's line of thought: Children surrounded by angelic guard are not to be offended, because they always have angelic guard watching over [them], [which guard] always has the present face of the heavenly Father, and thus [they have a guard as] perpetual defense against offenses and offenders.

[We prove this thesis] (b) from Eph 3:10 "That now the manifold wisdom of God might be made known to principalities and powers in heaven by the church."

Observe (1). The case is clear that angels are meant by "principalities and powers." However, since not only good but also evil angels, below, Eph 6:12, are called "principalities" and "powers," the question is whether good or rather evil spirits are to be understood here. The Ambrosian commentary refers to the evil [angels], but the matter itself as well as the exposition of all interpreters, both ancient and more recent, demands that the good [angels] be understood.

Observe (2). It is said that that becomes known which previously was unknown. Hereby therefore the apostle declares that the knowledge and understanding also of the angels themselves is increased by the proclamation of the Gospel.

Observe (3). By "church" in this passage is not meant the heavenly or triumphant church, as Augustine would have it, but [the church] militant [that is] on earth and

[is] gathered from Gentiles and Jews. Chrysostom indeed says that Paul, the evangelist of the angels, here enlightened, that is instructed and taught, those [in the former], and Thomas[66] teaches from Cyril that, with Paul preaching, the angels learned the circumstances of the Gospel and of the call of the Gentiles. But not from the church as teacher,[67] but through the church, that is, through the things that are done in the church, did the angels learn this mystery in greater detail, namely that God would have not only Jews but also Gentiles saved, and free salvation is to be offered them in Christ. Therefore their knowledge could be increased.

Observe (4). The [Greek] word *poikilos* denotes variety. But not at all satisfied with that [word], the apostle calls the wisdom of God *polypoikilos*, manifold, or varied very much and in many ways, because of the marvelous variety that every creature justly admires, and [he] has in mind the admirable governance of the church.

[We prove this thesis] (c) from 1 Ptr 1:12: "Which things the angels desire to look into."

Observe (1). The Vulgate translates *in quem* [on whom], on basis of which some papists refer to the Holy Spirit, others to Christ.[68] But all Greek codices have *eis ha*, into which, namely mysteries of the Gospel, or of human salvation, foretold by the prophets and proclaimed to the world by the apostles.

Observe (2). The verb "look into" is used properly of those who diligently and, as it were, with inclined head and neck and with fixed eyes look attentively,[69] so that the matter might be known in greater detail; see Lk 24:12; Jn 20:4–5; Jas 1:25.

Observe (3). The apostle speaks not of the first step of cognition but of more abundant knowledge—in line with more circumstances—of things that were formerly known in part. The angels therefore so delight in the mysteries of the Gospel and of the kingdom of Christ, known by them earlier, that they desire to know them gradually more fully and more completely.

Thesis IX

Ectypal theology of mere human beings is partly of the way, or of this life—[and] this is also called [theology] of travelers—partly of home,[70] or of the other and blessed life—[and] this [is] also [called theology] of things obtained.

Note: It is called theology of the way and of travelers because by it people, while they are still situated on the way in this mortal state, are directed to the heavenly home and eternal blessedness to be obtained. It is called theology of home and of things obtained because finally, with the course of this life finished, they attain that [life] in the heavenly fatherland and, as it were, obtain the preset goal. Now, the names "life" and "travelers," "home" and "things obtained" are drawn from 1 Co 9:24 and 2 Co 5:6, 8. In the former, mention is made of those who run in a race, and they that run a race are exhorted so to run that they may obtain, namely the blessedness toward which they strive on their way even as toward a preset goal. In the latter, the believers, before attaining blessedness, are compared to travelers and pilgrims because, absent from the Lord [and] in a foreign land, they desire to depart from the body and go to dwell with the Lord.

Thesis X

Theology of the way or of the travelers is partly before the Fall, partly after the Fall. That which was before the Fall in the state of innocence is also called Paradisiacal, from the place in which man was situated. And this is again divided by reason of source[71] into concreate and revealed [theology].

Thesis XI

Concreate Paradisiacal theology, which is also call primitive or original, consisted in perfect inherent[72] knowledge of God, which was attached to the first-formed ones as a creation favor[73] by which they were made in the image of God.

Note: The form of primitive knowledge of God is a concreated quality.[74] By that very fact it is distinguished from actual[75] acquired wisdom of God. The subject or matter-in-which[76] is [our] first parents before the Fall. It was indeed intended also for all their descendants, but as it turned out[77] it did not exist except in the first-formed ones. Its source[78] was the grace of creation, by which they were made in the image of God. The material-about-which,[79] or primary object, was God the Creator; the secondary [object was] man himself and the other creatures. Hence the Lombard[80] reports that man before the Fall was endowed[81] with threefold knowledge: (1) of the things made for his sake; (2) of the Creator; and (3) of himself. This knowledge of Adam did not include: (1) the hidden decrees of God, which cannot be known without divine revelation, Ro 11:34; (2) future events, such as was the Fall itself, likewise the incarnation of the Son of God; (3) secrets of hearts and the inmost thoughts of angels and men: [and] (4) any and all kinds of individual things.[82]

The thesis is proved from Cl 3:10: "And putting on the new (man), who is renewed as to[83] knowledge, according to the image of Him who created him."

Observe: From this statement we reason thus: What we acquire by the new creation, that is, regeneration and renewal by the grace of the Holy Spirit, that Adam had in the first creation. And we acquire knowledge [KJV] in a new creation, that is, regeneration and renewal by the grace of the Holy Spirit. Therefore Adam had knowledge in the first creation. For renewal presupposes that that which is renewed was formerly present and later by old age[84] was either obliterated or altogether blotted out. And if the image of God consists in knowledge or cognition, Adam was surely created with it, for he was created in the image of God.

Thesis XII

Revealed Paradisiacal theology is the cognition that [our] first parents had before the Fall from divine revelation through the outward enunciative[85] Word, which [revelation] occurred at particular times[86] regarding various matters.

Note I. Divine revelation occurred (1) in the blessing of the first human beings and in granting [them] dominion over all living creatures, Gn 1:28; (2) in the designation of foods, vv. 29–30; (3) in the sanctification of the Sabbath, Gn 2:3; (4) in the proclamation of the law regarding abstaining from eating of the tree of the knowledge of good and evil, Gn 2:16–17; and (5) in the association of a life partner and of help, v. 18.

Note II. Distinguish between increate, concreate, and revealed theology. Increate [theology] belongs solely to God, by nature, and to the human nature of Christ because of the union. Concreate [theology] was indeed in Adam before the Fall and consisted in perfect inherent[87] knowledge of God, put into [our] first parents by virtue of creation, Cl 3:10. Hence it is also called primeval, original, and concreate theology, but the greatest part was lost by the Fall. But revealed [theology] began in the state before the Fall and it still remains in the church.

Note III. Franciscus Junius and Alsted make the theology of man in the incorrupt state twofold; natural and supernatural. But the theology of incorrupt man was rather part of the image of God, as is clear from 2 Co 3:18; Eph 4:24; Cl 3:10. But now the image of God in man before the Fall was not a supernatural but a natural gift. And Ec 7:29 testifies that God created man upright; and what man has in himself by primeval creation, that is his by nature, as will be more fully set forth in its place.

Note IV. Distinguish between Paradisiacal theology, or [theology] of primeval integrity, and Christian [theology] of gracious restoration. The former had its day before the Fall, the latter obtained after the Fall. The former is named after the place in which man was first situated, the latter after the chief object of consideration, namely Christ the Redeemer.

Note V. The theology of gracious restoration, or the restoration of mankind by the woman's seed that would crush the serpent's head, Gn 3:15, was indeed revealed also in Paradise, but after the Fall, since [our] first parents were then already banished from Paradise by the Law itself, because of transgression—dispossessed, though it was later that they were actually[88] banished after the proclamation of the Gospel.

Thesis XIII

The theology of those who are travelers and pilgrims [absent] from the Lord in the state after the Fall is either natural or supernatural (or revealed). Natural [knowledge of God] is drawn from the light of nature or from common impressed notions of the mind that are created[89] by observation of visible creatures. For God is known naturally, partly by notions implanted in us by nature, partly by traces of the invisible things of God impressed on created things, so that natural knowledge of God[90] is either implanted by way of a connate quality or acquired, Ro 1:19–20.

Note I. Let natural theology be considered either in its original wholeness or in [its] ruins and remains. In the former way it was evident[91] in Adam before the Fall and consisted in perfect inherent[92] concreate knowledge of God, which was discussed in Thesis XI. But if you consider it in the latter way, namely considered in [its] ruins and remains, there indeed remained in corrupt nature after the Fall some knowledge of God and [of] the divine law, but weak, imperfect, and by no means sufficient for salvation.

Note II. Natural theology[93] is of the same time of origin as [that of] man, and it antecedes supernatural [theology].

Note III. As after the conflagration of a splendid house ashes and burnt particles, or after the collapse of a building with a very great fall some ruins remain, so also some weak remains and fragments of the divine image and small sparks of the primeval light that shone in the mind of man before the Fall remain in fallen and miserably prostrate nature. Hence Augustine [says]: "What was impressed in the mind through the image of God when [man] was created was not altogether destroyed."

Note IV. This world is not only like a teacher, a witness, [and] preacher, but also a book, a theater, [and] mirror in which God shows not only His deity but also His benefactions toward us and our obligation toward Him, to be read and contemplated, in fact to be touched, as it were, Ro 1:19–20; Acts 17:27.

Note V. Moreover implanted reason, stirred up by thought[94] and the inclination of the will to observe what is true, by its own natural light, is like an eye reading and contemplating, Ro 1:20, by apprehension of simple things, combination[95] and division, reasoning and sorting things out.[96]

Thesis XIV

Supernatural or revealed theology, which arises out of the light of grace, is in one way [theology] of direct revelation or inspiration, in another way [theology] of indirect manifestation or institution. The former befell the prophets, apostles, and evangelists by inspiration of God and direct afflatus of the Holy Spirit and illumination or irradiation, and it is no longer given in the church. The latter is drawn from the Word of God revealed and set down in writing, and it still flourishes in the church.

Thesis XV

Revealed theology, or [theology] drawn from the revealed and written Word, is the knowledge of God and of divine things that God communicates to mankind in this life through the revelation made in the Word for the praise of His glorious grace and [for] the salvation of mankind.

Note I. (1) It is called supernatural theology because it is not drawn out of principles of nature but is drawn from oracles of Scripture and transcends our ability to understand. And it is rightly called supernatural for this reason, that it is above, not contrary to, nature and cannot conflict with the truth. (2) It is called theology of the way or of travelers and, in the apostolic term, the Way, Acts 19:9 and 23, [and] the way of the Lord, Acts 18:26, because it is the theology of people who walk by faith and who are directed on the way and [on the] journey to the heavenly fatherland by the light of grace kindled in the Word. (3) It is called abstractive theology because we know God in this life by an abstract concept[97] or by the mirror of the Word, 1 Co 13:12, not by [His] essence. (4) Finally [theology is called] revealed, or [theology] of mediate revelation because it is drawn from the revelation of the divine Word. By Franciscus Junius and Alsted it is called humble theology and our [theology], by others the theology of the church militant.

Note II. Revealed theology is taken (1) broadly for the [theology] that acknowledges for [its] source in general the revelation or manifestation of God, be that made either through nature or through Scripture, that is, through the singular grace in the Word. [It is taken] (2) strictly for the [theology] that rests solely on the divine revelation made in the Word and embraces the whole doctrine of God and [of] the other divine mysteries revealed in Scripture; and this is [the theology] of this topic. For it is called revealed theology after revelation—not the general [revelation] that makes that which may be known of God known to the minds of men partly by implanted notions, partly by things done by God, Ro 1:19–20, but after the special revelation by which the things that are necessary for us to know for salvation about God and His worship have been manifested in a supernatural way in the written Word through men inspired by God.

Note III. Natural theology, which remained left over after the Fall, differs from supernatural or revealed [theology] (1) by reason of the source. In the former the source is reason, or the light of nature, in the latter [it is] the revelation made in the Word, or Holy Scripture. [It differs] (2) by reason of form: The form of the former is knowledge, but of the latter [it is] faith. [It differs] (3) by reason of matter: Natural theology is occupied with a little particle, namely about the existence, power, and righteousness of God and the function of the Law, Ro 1:20; 2:15. Revealed theology contains the perfect knowledge of God, of Law and Gospel, [and] of sin and of Christ, and teaches all things that are necessary to us for salvation. [It differs] (4) by reason of purpose: Only revealed theology leads to life eternal. Natural [theology] does not suffice thereto; in fact it also does not contribute anything toward obtaining it.

We prove this very thing (I) from 1 Co 13:9: "We know in part, and we prophecy in part"; v. 12: "For now we see by a mirror in an obscure way." [We prove it] (II) from 2 Co 5:6–7: "While we are in the body, we are absent from the Lord (for we walk by faith, not by sight)."

Observe (1). The term "in part" denotes the imperfection of our knowledge in this world; hence also "that which is perfect" is used in contrast to it, 1 Co 13:10, and of that the apostle says in the preceding v. 8: "Knowledge will pass away," that is, the imperfection of knowledge (both that which consists in the very nature of knowing and that which [consists in] the nature of acquiring) will cease in the life to come,[98] with the clear and perfect vision and knowledge of God following, which the apostle expressly sets over against part knowledge, v. 12, saying, "Now I know in part, but then I will know even as also I am known."

Observe (2). The apostle compares the Word of God with a mirror. Now, in the use of a mirror two things are usually considered, the face and its image. Of these, the former presents itself, the latter is presented. The latter we call an image, the former [we call] the archetype. So the mirror portrays and presents to the beholders an image of a thing, not the thing itself or prototype. Thus Heinsius[99] on Jas 1:23. Others say: A mirror presents a thing itself to the eyes not directly and as it is in itself but as it were by reflected rays and therefore more obscurely and less perfectly than if the thing were seen in itself and directly. Thus Cornelius a Lapide, Menochius,[100] Tirinus,[101] [and] others. Such a mirror, namely in which we can contemplate divine things, God set before us (1) in nature and created things, in which as it were some gleam of divinity shines, Ro 1:20. [God set it before us] (2) in Scripture, which shows us God and divine things so far as is necessary to attain salvation. The meaning therefore is: Just as in a mirror we do not observe physical things directly and as they are in themselves but only their images and likenesses and therefore we behold those things imperfectly, so also do we not behold God directly and in Himself in this life but as it were His image, revealed in the Word, and therefore [we behold Him] imperfectly.

Observe (3). It increases the imperfection, because the apostle adds "dimly." Now, all our knowledge, in this life, about God and divine mysteries is called clouded not because it is uncertain or fallacious, obscure, and confused, but because it is less clear and perfect if it is compared with that which is to come in the life to come.

Observe (4). The apostle divides the knowledge of God into that of a mirror, or abstractive, [and] direct, or intuitive, and by the particles "now" and "then" he explains to which state of life each pertains.

Observe (5). In 2 Co 5:6 ff. faith and sight are set over against each other, "for we walk by faith, not by sight"; that is, the state of the gracious indwelling of God and of faith, or the vision by faith, is set over against the state of the vision of God by sight. The former is of this life, the latter of the other life. Hence Gregory [says]: "The things that are seen, then, do not have faith but knowledge." And Augustine: "This is faith, to believe what you do not see." "To walk by faith," therefore, is not yet to behold and see God and Christ face to face, but only to know by faith, which has as its counterobject[102] Christ, invisible to us in this world and absent in this way, that is, not yet visible; and hence we say: "We are absent from the Lord."

Thesis XVI

The theology of indirect revelation, or of institution, is either catechetic, initial, or more elementary (which is also called [theology] of babes,[103] of novices and beginners) or profound,[104] advanced, or more detailed (which is also called [theology] of the mature[105] [or] established).

Thesis XVII

Catechetic theology is that which singles out only the chief heads of Christian doctrine and trains the unlearned common people in them. Hence it is also called elementary or initial, because it teaches the first elements and rudiments of the Christian religion and is chiefly concerned with laying the foundations of the doctrine of faith. This kind of teaching was once called catechesis and catechism, the teachers themselves were called catechists, the learners[106] [were called] catechumens, [and] the action itself was called instruction or catechization, 1 Co 14:19; Gl 6:6; Acts 18:25.

We prove this thesis from Heb 5:12: "You that, by reason of the time, needed to be teachers, need to be taught again what are the elementary principles of the oracles of God, and you have become such as need milk and not solid food"; v. 13: "He whose thing is milk does not have the skill of the word of righteousness, for he is an infant."

Observe: The apostle calls catechetic theology (1) "the first principles of the oracles of God" and means the chief rudiments of Christianity, the first principles of faith, which are set before children and the more unlearned, the beginning doctrine, the ABC's of the divine Word, the elements, beginnings, and initial things. (2) The same elementary doctrine suitable for the unlearned who are to be initiated he calls milk (Peter calls it "pure milk," 1 Ptr 2:2) and at the same time he points out the salutary teats from which catechetic milk is to be drawn, namely the "oracles of God," evidently Holy Scripture, Ro 3:2; Acts 7:38. The subject for which milk is suited are[107] "they that need milk," Heb 5:12, that is, infants, v. 13, namely they who are infants in regard to knowledge of the more sublime mysteries, Heb 6:1. (3) He calls catechetic doctrine the "word of the beginning of the Christ, namely by which new Christians are initiated or at first trained; likewise "foundations." Now, "to lay [the] foundation" is to begin to teach and discuss the rudiments of the Christian faith. A parallel passage is 1 Co 3:1–2: "As unto babes in Christ. I fed you with milk to drink, and not solid food, for you were yet ready [for the latter] (namely to digest solid food), and even now you are not ready."

Thesis XVIII

Acroamatic theology is that which teaches [and] establishes the mysteries of faith in greater detail and at greater length and refutes errors against sound doctrine, and it is [the theology] of the bishops and presbyters in the church, and especially of those who in the schools teach not simply Christians but future teachers of Christians and are called chief theologians.

Note: Catechetic theology differs from acroamatic not in the matter considered but by reason of the object and way of considering [it]. The matter considered is the same in both cases, for in both cases divine matters and mysteries of the faith are taught. But the way of considering them is different. For the object of instruction in catechetic theology is a neophyte, catechumen Christian, unlearned in the doctrine of faith. In acroamatic [theology] it is a Christian who has already grown in the school of grace or has laid the first elements or foundations of faith. The object of doctrine of catechetic theology are[108] the chief heads of the Christian religion, the first elements of faith. In acroamatic theology they are the topics and headings of all theological matters. In the former the purpose or end is summary knowledge of the heavenly doctrine; in the latter it is fuller and more detailed understanding.

This thesis is proved from the passage just now cited, namely from Heb 5:12: "You that needed" etc.

Observe: Just as in this passage "milk" is the easier and lower doctrine, which is suited for the unlearned and immature,[109] as said, so "solid food" is the higher and fuller explanation of the divine mysteries, suited for the instructed and more mature. Hence the apostle says in the following v. 14: "Solid food is for those who are of full age (that is, for the mature, who have learned well the articles of the Christian religion and have made praiseworthy progress in the word of righteousness etc.). In Heb 6:1 he calls the same fuller knowledge of Christian doctrine "perfection," and he sets it over against "the word of the beginning of the Christ and [against] the foundation of faith." Compare 1 Co 3:2.

Thesis XIX

In regard to manner of presentation, acroamatic theology is either exegetic, or didactic strictly so called, or polemic, or homiletic, or casual,[110] or finally historical.

Thesis XX

Exegetic theology, which [is] also Biblical, also called prophetic by some, is that which is concerned with a paraphrase or a fuller explanation and commentary[111] on either the whole or part of Holy Scripture, a book or some passage of it, and investigates its truth and true meaning.

Thesis XXI

Didactic theology, strictly so called, which is also called systematic and thetic or positive, is that which sets forth in order and clearly explains the theological commonplaces, exactly defines and divides the doctrines of faith, and derives and proves them from the fundamental seat that they have in Holy Scripture.

Note: This didactic theology is suited to schools and academies and is much more detailed and fuller than the popular or catechetical [theology] that obtains in the churches among the unlearned people. Here the truth of things, beauty of words, and clarity of method ought to obtain. Here are taught definitions of theological matters or of articles of faith, causes, relations, divisions, likes, dislikes, etc.

Thesis XXII

Polemic theology, polemic and controversial, or controversial and refutative, which others call scholastic, or rather academic, deals with ancient and more recent theological controversies, properly formulates the point of the question, establishes the heavenly truth with arguments drawn from Holy Scripture, defends established [truth] against objections, asserts vindicated [truth] against objections and is thus concerned with building up orthodoxy and tearing down heterodoxy or in building up the truth and destroying falsehood. Briefly: Didactic theology teaches the truth, polemic [theology] defends the truth.

Note I. Didactic and controversial theology do not differ in regard to matter but only as to the way of handling [it].

Note II. In polemic theology this is especially to be avoided, that idle questions be piled up and arguments grow out of arguments, thus creating a theology of strife and contention, in which the truth is lost by too much altercation.

Thesis XXIII

Homiletic theology, which they also call ecclesiastic, revolves around the manner of preaching and the practice of public speaking and chiefly teaches future ministers of the church. But at the same time, speaking accurately, how a teacher should learn to handle divine things does not constitute a special theology, nor some principal part, but belongs to the article on the ministry of the church, as blessed Calov, my colleague, fellow countryman,[112] and highly distinguished and very close brother in Christ, well observes.

Thesis XXIV

Casual theology or [theology] of cases, which some also call consistorial, deals with the things that they do for conscience, or to instruct conscience in doubtful cases, so that it either be raised up if [it is] weak, or set right and corrected if [it is] in error, or resolved if [it is] doubtful and has scruples; or, which is the same, is concerned about doubtful cases of conscience to be decided on the basis of the Word of God. Its purpose therefore is to decide cases of doubt or of scruples and questions of conscience, or of courses of action.[113]

Thesis XXV

Historic theology is that which tells the history of the ancient or primitive church and sets forth how in it the doctrine of the Gospel was propagated by the orthodox, attacked by heretics, [and] defended not only by councils but also by teachers in [their] speaking and writings.

Thesis XXVI

Theology of the homeland or of the blessed, which others call intuitive or [theology] of sight, is the knowledge of God and of divine things communicated by God to the blessed in the life to come by a clear vision of the divine essence, so that, enjoying this supreme blessedness, they glorify the eternal God.

Note I. One must distinguish between theology of the way or of revelation and [theology] of life or of sight; or between theology communicated by gracious revelation to the church militant on earth and [theology] communicated by glorious vision to the church triumphant in heaven, that is, the angels and the blessed. The former is also called apprehensive theology or [theology] of the way; the latter [is also called] comprehensive, or [theology] of the goal and homeland; the former is transient, the latter permanent; the former is imperfect (for all our progress in the knowledge and wisdom of God in this life, also when it reaches the highest step, is a defective statement whose close is, "The remaining things are lacking," says my uncle, Johann Gerhard), the latter [is] perfect; the former serves as the middle, the latter as the end; the former is of this miserable life, the other of the next and blessed life.

Note II. It is called (1) theology of sight because it consists in clear and intuitive vision and knowledge of God. (2) [It is called] theology of life because it befalls the blessed in eternal life. (3) [It is called] theology of the homeland and of things obtained, not with regard to adequate knowledge, but with regard to obtaining the desired end, 1 Co 9:24. (4) [It is called] highest theology, [theology] of the blessed, of the church triumphant, etc. The form of this theology is clear, intuitive knowledge, face to face. [Its] end is the very knowledge of God connected with full enjoyment. Its effect: It makes people confirmed in bliss and partakers of all good things. Its subject are[114] the angels, blessed souls, and saved people.

We prove this thesis (a) from the words of Christ, Mt 5:8: "Blessed [are] the pure in heart, for they shall see God"; (b) from 1 Co 13:12: "We see by a mirror in an obscure way, but then face to face"; 1 Jn 3:2: "Now, we know that when He will appear we will be like Him, for we will see Him as He is."

Observe (1). They whose hearts have been purified by faith, Acts 15:9, who are of simple and sincere heart, [and] who strive to keep the heart clean from the filth of vices, evil desires, [and] wicked intents will see God, here with enlightened eyes, as in an obscure way, by a mirror, [and] hereafter face to face.

Observe (2). 1 Co 13:12 and 1 Jn 3:2 it is said that we will not only see God, as in Mt 5:8 and Heb 12:14, but that we will see face to face and as He is. Now, "face to face" is a figurative term, for God does not properly have a face or countenance (as the anthropomorphites believe, deceived by an elementary and crass error), but by that periphrasis is denoted that bright and completely clear vision of the divine essence, and what Paul calls "vision face to face" St. John explains by personal vision. For the blessed will behold the divine essence clearly, perfectly, not through figures, [but] directly—so far as the infinity of divine majesty and the limitations of human minds permit.

Observe (3). The phrase "to see God face to face" has a twofold meaning in the Scriptures: (1) It denotes a vision and remarkable view of the Son of God in human form, or another form assumed for a time, or also a friendly and familiar association of God with man, which vision can befall man also in this life and in fact did befall the patriarch Jacob, Gn 32:30, [and] Moses, Ex 33:11; Nm 12:8; Dt 34:10.—(2) It means a clear and intuitive vision of the divine essence, different from the vision of this life not only in degrees but also in this life. For it is "the highest reward of the blessed," as Augustine testifies, "the reward of faith that is kept for us in the life to come."

Thesis XXVII

Moreover, the word theology is taken either in a wide sense or in a narrow sense. In a wide sense it is taken for the whole doctrine of God and divine things; and in a narrow sense [it is taken] for the part of heavenly doctrine that deals either with God, one in essence and trine in persons, or also teaches the divinity of the only Son of God. Hence among the Greek fathers *theologein ton logon* is to assert and confess the divinity of Christ. Hence also arose the distinction of the ancients between theology and economy or dispensation. The former denotes to the Greeks the doctrine of divinity, the latter either [the doctrine] of the incarnation and humanity of the Son of God or of the dispensation and restoration of man wrought by Christ.

Note: The Greek fathers usually separate from economy or dispensation the doctrine of God properly so called, which they particularly call theology and sometimes simple theology, as Horn[115] testifies. Thus Eusebius, bishop of Caesarea in Palestine, distinguishes in Christ the theology according to Himself, that is, [His] divinity and profession of divinity, and the descent from heaven to us, that is, the incarnation. Basil the Great says: "It does not teach us the manner of theology but manifests the doctrine of dispensation."

Thesis XXVIII

Finally, the word theology is taken either essentially, absolutely, and by way of nature for the knowledge that is known in the mind and inheres in the heart of man or insofar as it is a quality of the heart,[116] or accidentally, relatedly,[117] [and] systematically, insofar as it is doctrine or discipline that is taught and learned or is contained in books. The former meaning[118] of the word is primary, the latter [is] secondary. For theology is principally called a theological aptitude,[119] but secondarily and less principally doctrine, statement, or also a book and system presenting theology.

Thesis XXIX

Theology viewed systematically and abstractively is the doctrine built from the Word of God by which people are instructed in true faith and pious life unto life eternal, or it is the doctrine drawn from divine revelation that points out how people are to be taught about the worship of God through Christ unto life eternal.

Note: In the place of genus we put teaching, instruction, or doctrine. For theology is set forth and learned by teaching. Moses, Dt 32:2, Solomon, Pr 8:10, Jeremiah, Jer. 3:15, Christ Himself, Jn 7:16–17, [and] the apostles, Acts 2:42 [and] 1 Ti 1:10, use this general term. The form and norm of this doctrine is Sacred Scripture. The object is the revealed worship of God through Christ. The end is life eternal [and] the glory of God.

Thesis XXX

Theology considered as an aptitude and concretively is a God-given practical aptitude of the understanding, conferred through the Word by the Holy Spirit on man, regarding true religion, so that by His work man, a sinner, might be brought through faith in Christ to God and eternal salvation.

Note I. This meaning of the word theology is [that] of this topic. For here we consider theology not significatively, as it is in a book, but subjectively, as it is in the heart. For the name "theologians" is derived from [the word] "theology," the form, as it were, giving the name and the subject inhering.

Note II. The remote genus of theology we call aptitude, namely intellectual, or one that perfects our mind; the proximate [genus we call] an aptitude given by God, namely through the written Word; we say furthermore that it is a practical aptitude, on which more in Section II, Polemic.

Thesis XXXI

The principle efficient cause of theology is the Triune God, for He that is the highest author of the revealed Word is also the principal cause of theology, which is drawn from the revealed Word. For "whatever is to be understood about God is to be learned from God," says Hilary.[120]

This thesis is proved from Ja 1:5: "If any of you lack wisdom, let him ask of God, who gives liberally to all"; v. 17: "Every good gift and every perfect gift is from above, coming down from the Father of lights."

Observe (1). The particle "if" in this passage is not of one doubting but of one supposing: If any lack, that is, whereas or because, since anyone lacks wisdom; for by nature we are all unwise and ignorant, Acts 17:30, not perceiving, not knowing the "things that are of the Spirit of God," 1 Co 2:14.

Observe (2). By the word "wisdom" the apostle means not philosophic but theological wisdom, namely (a) in general, knowledge of the mysteries of faith and of salvation, [and] (b) in particular, wisdom in adversities to be endured not only patiently but also with joy, Ja 1:2. Hence Balthasar Baes,[121] Lusitanian teacher, explains "wisdom" in this passage as "prudent wisdom, to temper the bitterness of tribulations."

Observe (3). Some hold that the little term "to all" is to be taken in a narrow sense, namely of all who ask properly and desire this wisdom in the proper way, since it is immediately added, v. 6: "But let him ask in faith, disputing nothing." Others take it indiscriminately of all, since God is so generous a giver that He does good not only to the good but also to the evil, Mt 5:45, and [since] there is expressly added the particle "freely, without reservation," which is to be connected not with the word "gives" but with "to all," so that the sense is: God gives to all without exception, that is, to all without any respect of persons, as Thomas, Brochmand, Laurentius, [and] others explain.

Observe (4). As God is the source of all good and perfect things, as it is said in Ja 1:17, so He is also the only giver of wisdom. Hence also the same [that is, wisdom] is called "wisdom that comes from above or from heaven," Ja 3:15. "He gives a spirit of wisdom and revelation in the knowledge of Him," Eph 1:17.

Thesis XXXII

The moving cause of revealed theology is either initiating and internal or immediate exciting and external. The former is the boundless goodness and inexhaustible mercy of God, by which God, as it were the highest good especially communicative of itself, deigned to impart His wisdom to men and, coming forth out of the hidden seat of His majesty, to reveal Himself to mankind. The latter is both our ignorance of divine things and [our] inevitable misery after the Fall, by which [ignorance and misery] we would have perished forever if God, having mercy on us, had not brought us to know Him by His revealed Word.

Thesis XXXIII

The mediating cause[122] of theology is the written Word of God. We know nothing of the divine mysteries but by divine revelation comprehended in the Sacred Scriptures. In fact, the written Word of God is that "incorruptible seed," of which the church is born and sacred and holy theology is perfected, 1 Ptr 1:23, 25.

Note: Blessed König[123] calls the written Word of God the instrumental cause of theology, but this must be knowledgeably understood. The Word of God can indeed be called an organ or instrument of theology, but in a wider sense and especially with regard to the material, namely the outward writing, preaching, dispensing, and ministry, but not properly and accurately, namely with regard to the formal, that is to say the inspiration of God, and of the Spirit's internal power and efficacy communicated by the Holy Word. The Word of God is "the power of God unto salvation to everyone who believes," Ro 1:16. But to call the power of God communicated inwardly by the Word an instrument is for us a religious offense.[124]

Thesis XXXIV

Ministerial causes of theology are (1) The writers directly inspired by God, that is, the prophets in the Old [Testament] and the evangelists and apostles in the New Testament. (2) The orthodox teachers and ministers of the church, 1 Co 12:28 ff.; Eph 4:11. Basil the Great briefly summarizes these causes of theology, saying: "The Lord taught thus, the apostles preached, [and] the pastors preserved."[125]

Thesis XXXV

The form of theology is gathered from its genus, and the specific difference is drawn from the other causes. Now, there is (1) a remote genus, namely the intellectual aptitude, or that which perfects our intellect, (2) a near [genus], namely the practical aptitude, and (3) the nearest [genus], namely the practical aptitude given by God, or conferred on man by the Holy Spirit through the Word.

Thesis XXXVI

The matter of which theology consists are the theological truths (as the scholastics call them), that is, the theological principles and conclusions drawn from the revealed Word as from the proper principle. The matter-about-which, or the object, is God, revealed in the Word, and all divine things.

Thesis XXXVII

The subject of theology is for one thing that of inhesion or denomination, for another that of discussion, [and] for another that of operation. The subject of inhesion is twofold, what and by what. The "what" subject is man the theologian, or one who is equipped with the ability of theology, the man of God, 2 Ti 3:17. The "by what" subject is the mind and intellect of him in whom the ability of theology is directly. The subject of discussion, or of consideration, or, as they say, the general object, are all things theological, or divinely revealed, insofar as they are to be perceived by us to attain salvation, which things are comprehended by the one term "true religion." The subject of operation is man after the Fall, or man the sinner, as[126] available for salvation[127] or to be instructed and brought to life eternal. It is called subject of operation because the theological aptitude revolves around this, that it might introduce its end therein through certain means.

Thesis XXXVIII

The purpose of theology is twofold, intermediate and final. The intermediate [purpose] is either outward or inward. The outward intermediate purpose is saving faith; the inward [intermediate purpose] is the action and operation of a theologian to attain that end, that is, [action] directed [to] bring man the sinner to faith and life eternal, or it is any function of a theologian acting to generate or increase or strengthen the faith and to look after the salvation of people. The final purpose of theology is such either absolutely or in a certain respect. The final purpose, absolutely, is glory or glorification and fruition of God. The final purpose in a certain respect is the eternal salvation of people, or rather bringing [people] to eternal salvation, Jn 20:31. For, accurately speaking, the end of faith is eternal salvation as such, and the purpose of theology is bringing man to salvation.

Section II

Polemic

Question I

Is theology given?

The Point at Issue

The question here is not (1) regarding the false theology of devils or of those misled by the devil, but regarding true theology; (2) not regarding archetypal, infinite, and essential theology; but regarding ectypal, finite, and accidental [theology]; (3) not regarding ectypal theology of the human nature of Christ or of the good angels, but of mere human beings; (4) not regarding increate theology (such as is in God) or concreate [theology] (such as was in Adam before the Fall), but revealed [theology]; (5) not regarding Paradisiacal theology and [theology] of primeval integrity, but the Christian theology and [theology] of the gracious restoration; (6) not regarding the theology of sight and life, but [the theology] of revelation and of the way; (7) not regarding the theology of direct inspiration, but [the theology] of indirect instruction; (8) finally, not regarding natural theology, but supernatural [theology].

Thesis

Revealed or supernatural theology, or the doctrine of God and divine things drawn from the written Word of God, by which sinful people are instructed in true faith and pious life unto life eternal, is given in the church, militant in this world.

Exposition

Note I. In Section I, Didactic, we offered an explanation of the terms of which mention was made in the Point at Issue.

Note II. Under the name "revealed theology" we include catechetic and acroamatic theology, and so also exegetic, didactic, polemic, homiletic, casual,[128] and historical theology.

Antithesis

I. Of the atheists, who, as they deny that God exists, so they also reject the knowledge of God, or theology.

II. Of the pagans, or Gentiles, who, as they do not admit the source of theology, namely the revealed Word of God, so [they] also [do not admit] the authoritative teaching, that is, theology itself drawn from the Word of God.

III. Of the freethinkers, who, by denying that God teaches us through the outward Word and admitting only the inner Spirit, consequently call into question theology itself, built on the outward Word—as the Schwenkfelders, Enthusiasts, Paracelsists, and Weigelians, and other fanatics who, as they reject the whole written Word of God and attribute all things to hidden raptures and inner afflatuses or enthusiasms, so also reject theology, schools, and academies, to whom add David Joris, Hendrik Niclaes, etc.

Confirmation of the Thesis

Our thesis is proved I. from the efficient cause posited in the act, namely God speaking to us in His Word, or divine revelation itself, which is the source of theology; and with the efficient cause imbedded[129] in the act, the effect is established.[180] With divine revelation admitted, it is impossible to be in doubt regarding theology, which rests on it, as to whether it is given.

[Our thesis is proved] II. from the purpose of man, which is life eternal. Jn 3:17: "God did not send [His] Son into the world to condemn the world, but that the world might be saved through Him."

Note I. The goal of the mission of the Son of God is indicated (1) by the negative,[131] "not to judge the world." "The world" are all people living in the world; to "judge" is to condemn because of sin and to deliver up to hell. (2) By the positive,[132] "but that the world might be saved through Him." "To be saved" is to be brought from sins to righteousness, from Satan to God, from hell to heaven. For the word "save" does not mean only the end of faith, namely eternal salvation itself, but also the means ordained to that end and the whole order of salvation to be obtained established[183] by God.

Note II. Now, to this end (namely life eternal) no one is brought or can aspire without the special revelation that is set forth in theology. Therefore either no one pursues this end, ordained by God, or, if man ought to pursue [it], revealed theology, as the medium suited and necessary to attain that end, must be given, since one cannot aspire thereto through the natural knowledge of God.

[Our thesis is proved] III. from the material cause. For many things are given that cannot be known through nature and yet are truly known about God and divine things, knowledge of which must not be ascribed but to divine revelation made in the Word. Therefore some revealed theology is certainly given. The preceding is clear from the introduction of the articles of faith regarding the Trinity, Christ, predestination, [and] justification, as our blessed Calov well teaches.

[Our thesis is proved] IV. from the consensus of all peoples. For though the Gentiles outside the church have for the most part wandered away from true theology, they have, by [their] zeal of pursuing it, proved that it exists. And no people is found that might subsist only by the light of nature in things that pertain to religion and divine worship, and not reject, though falsely, some revelations received from God.

[Our thesis is proved] V. from the examples of theologians. Theologians are given, therefore also theology. For with the concrete and the denominated subject established, the abstract and denominating form is also established.

Sources of Rebuttals,[184] or Dialysis of Objections

I. Observe: Though theology or knowledge of divine things is conferred by the Holy Spirit and is "the wisdom that comes from above" or from heaven, Ja 3:15, and "a gift coming down from the Father of lights," Ja 1:17, yet it is not bestowed directly, but through Holy Scripture; hence the Holy Spirit commends him who loves to search or study it, Jn 5:39. And the school of the Holy Spirit does not reject all information, book, ink, paper, [and] pen (as the Enthusiasts and Weigelians do) but requires labor in earnest and condemns indolence and idle raptures.

II. Though toward the beginning of the very young church the Holy Spirit miraculously poured out on the apostles and other believers the gifts of tongues, wisdom, and knowledge, yet nevertheless also the apostles themselves in the school of Christ were moreover uninstructed for some years and received these very gifts extraordinarily from the Holy Spirit to this end, that they might be able to instruct others through ordinary means of teaching.

III. Though the apostle Paul, in the third heaven, was instructed in the mysteries of the Christian religion, yet nevertheless he wanted "the books and parchments left behind with Carpus," 2 Ti 4:13. He wrote various letters to churches and their bishops in order to teach. He commanded to "give attendance to reading," 1 Ti 4:13, and to "labor in the Word and doctrine," that is, especially and hard and with weariness, 1 Ti 5:17 etc.

Question II

Is revealed theology necessary in the church?

The Point at Issue

The question is not (1) regarding an aptitude of faith but regarding an aptitude of conclusions or of theology; (2) not regarding any kind of and simple knowledge of the doctrines of faith but of an excellent and accurate knowledge of divine things; (3) the question is not whether it is necessary with respect to all members of the church, but whether [it is necessary] for the whole body of the church; (4) nor is the question about absolute but about hypothetical necessity.

Thesis

There is necessary in the church not only catechetic and more elementary theology, as without which God can neither be rightly known and worshiped nor life eternal obtained, but also acroamatic and more detailed [theology].

Exposition

I. Observe: It is not enough to know whether a thing exists; it is also required that it be known whether it is necessary; for these are different. Many things are allowed that are not allowed necessarily. Also wicked people and hypocrites are allowed in the church, but the church can do without them and in fact would have done without them if man had continued in [his] primeval state. Thus wars are allowed in the world, but they are not allowed necessarily. Sin [is allowed] in man, but not necessarily, for it is possible for it to have been lacking from human nature. But theology is given in the church, and it is given necessarily.

II. Distinguish between the aptitude of faith by which articles of faith necessary for salvation are believed and the aptitude of conclusions drawn[185] from Holy Scripture, by which doctrines of faith are set forth before others, explained from the Scriptures, confirmed, and defended against heretics. The aptitude of faith is improperly and rarely called theology, since it belongs indiscriminately to all believers, also the uneducated and unlearned, yet no one has called them theologians. But the latter, namely the aptitude of conclusions drawn from Scripture is properly and usually called theology and is a quality[186] of teachers of the church. For those who rightly acknowledge and worship the Triune God, as He has revealed Himself in His Word, are called believers, [but] not also theologians unless they can also draw from the Word of God, explain, confirm, and defend against enemies the things that belong to the salutary knowledge and worship of God. "It is one thing," says Augustine, "to know only what man ought to believe in order to attain the blessed life, but it is another thing to know how this very thing both helps the pious and is defended against the impious."

III. Distinguish between simple knowledge of divine things and wisdom of divine things, or that excellent and accurate knowledge of the divine will and of the mysteries. The former is required in all Christians and is necessary for all who are to be saved, as that without which no one can obtain salvation, Is 54:13; Jer 31:34; Jn 6:45. The latter belongs to the teachers of the church.

IV. Distinguish between catechetic or elementary theology and profound or more detailed [theology]; see Theses XVI, XVII, and XVIII of the preceding section. The former is required in all ministers of the Word and is necessary in each particular church, Ro 10:14. But the latter belongs to bishops and presbyters and especially academic teachers, who instruct the more accomplished ones.

V. Distinguish between that which is necessary for the church as the whole communion of Christians, and that which is necessary for the church as consisting of individual members. In the former way, theology is necessary at all events, Ro 10:14, but in the latter way [it is] not. 1 Co 12:29: "Are all teachers?" etc. It is not necessary that any and all believers be theologians, but that their teachers and leaders [be theologians].

VI. Distinguish between absolute and hypothetical necessity. Theology is not necessary absolutely and without reservation, not even for the whole church, for God can teach and convert people directly, that is, without the ministry of people who are theologians, but [theology is necessary] by hypothesis, namely with the will of God given. For it pleased God to deal with us through the Word and the preaching of it, Ro 10:14, and studying it, Jn 5:39, and to bring people to salvation through teaching and instruction. (I pointedly say, "Without the ministry of people who are theologians," for "directly" can be understood either of the ministry of people or of the proclamation of the Word; for in this way[187] God never directly converts anyone, but in that way[188] very often.)

VII. Distinguish between that which is necessary by necessity of precept, or that which is necessary to obtain the end because it is commanded by God, and that which is necessary by necessity of means. Each necessity is valid here.

Antithesis

Of the Enthusiasts, Schwenkfelders, Weigelians, and other fanatics, who hold that theology built on the outward Word is not necessary; God can instruct people unto eternal salvation by inward afflatuses, direct revelations, and angelic communications.

Confirmation of the Thesis

We take the proof of the thesis I. from the statements of Scripture. Lk 16:29: "They have Moses and the prophets; let them hear them." "But how will they hear without a preacher?" Ro 10:14. By these words we are taught that the ordinary means of faith and of becoming thoroughly acquainted with the Holy Scriptures is the ecclesiastical ministry, which consists of theologians.

[We take the proof of the thesis] II. from the nature of the source. Man is ordained by God to know and worship Him. But that knowledge and worship can be had from no other discipline than the theological.

[We take the proof of the thesis] III. from the nature of the end, namely of life eternal, to which only theology points the way. For theology is the knowledge of the way by which one not only surely attains eternal happiness but without which one cannot attain it.

[We take the proof of the thesis] IV. from the inability of natural theology, which shows that supernatural and revealed theology is necessary besides this.

Sources of Rebuttals or Dialysis of Objections

I. Observe on the passage [in] Jer 31:34: "They will teach no more every man his neighbor. . . . All will know Me, from the least of them even to the greatest," that the statement here is not about the direct revelation of the Word but of the knowledge of God in the time of the New Testament, both clearer with regard to the objects, 2 Ti 1:10, and richer and wider with regard to subjects, Ro 16:26; Eph 2:12–13. For these things are not to be understood in an absolute way, but comparatively, in comparison with the times of the Old Testament, to intimate the future worldwide preaching of the heavenly doctrine and likewise the greatness of the church and the fuller and easier knowledge of God in the time of the New Testament. And therefore that negative term, "will not teach," is elliptic, to be supplied by "not only," as in Gn 38:28; 1 Sm 8:7; Eze 16:47; Acts 5:4; Eph 6:12; etc., so that the meaning is: Not only, then, will there be a human ministry among men, but divine instruction will take precedence, as blessed Dorsche teaches.

II. Observation on that [statement] in Is 54:13: "They will all be taught by the Lord," which words are repeated [in] Jn 6:45. Reply: (1) Those words are not to be taken absolutely and exclusively, namely that in the New Testament the outward ministry of the Word is to be completely abolished, but comparatively, namely that the future knowledge of God in the New Testament is richer and clearer than it was in the Old Testament, and that the number of those might be greater who are endowed with a salutary knowledge of God in the New Testament than in the Old Testament, since the solemn and public preaching of the Word is no longer bound to one people but is common to all peoples. (2) Even if the reference here would be especially to direct revelation and instruction of God, yet it would not be necessary to admit those Enthusiastic raptures, since the words of the prophet can be explained of the Son of God Himself, who, as Heb 1:2 intimates, while He was visibly active on this earth, by direct act proclaimed the whole counsel of the Father regarding our salvation to people living at that time.

III. Observation on the passage in 1 Jn 2:27: "You have no need that anyone teach you; the same anointing teaches you concerning all things." That anointing was not obtained and is not now obtained through raptures, but through the Word of God, which "is Spirit and life," Jn 6:63, through which the Holy Spirit is imparted to us, Gl 3:2. That anointing is the Holy Spirit, the principal cause of faith, who teaches us not directly but by means of the Word, 1 Jn 2:14; 1 Th 2:13; Ro 10:17. And thus these words of the apostle are not to be understood absolutely or universally, as though it is not necessary for anyone at all to be taught by anyone, which conflicts with experience, which shows that after the Fall the knowledge of God is inborn in no person whatever, but [the words are to be understood] in a certain respect and comparatively, namely that they who were taught by the apostles regarding the necessary heads of heavenly doctrine and divinely imbued with the anointing of the Holy Spirit (for St. John speaks with such) do not need to hear or learn anything new from seducers. One gathers this interpretation from 1 Jn 2:21.

Question III

Is theology a God-given practical aptitude?

The Point at Issue

The question is not (1) regarding theology considered systematically, abstractively, and accidentally, but taken as an aptitude,[189] concretively, and essentially. (2) [The question is] not regarding an aptitude God-given by reason of direct infusion but by reason of invention,[140] principle, and object. (3) [The question is] not regarding a practical aptitude whose exercise is based on human power and revolves around human affairs, regarding which a philosopher [is concerned], but whose exercise is spiritual, namely bringing man to eternal salvation. (4) [The question is] not regarding a practical aptitude whose medium is the exercise or pursuit of good works, but which is so called because of the living exercise of faith, by which alone we aspire to life eternal. (5) [The question is] not regarding a practical aptitude that excludes all knowledge or at any rate presupposes any kind of it, but regards it with proper high regard,[141] yet does not finally rest on it and acquiesce [to] it.

Thesis

Theology is a God-given practical aptitude of the intellect given to man by the Holy Spirit through the written Word, regarding true religion, by which man after the Fall is to be brought to life eternal through faith in Christ.

Exposition

I. Observe: For the sake of a twofold way of consideration, the teachers assign a twofold genus to theology. For as it is considered systematically or insofar as it is contained in a book or writing, so its genus is doctrine, built from the Word of God; but insofar as it is considered concretively and as an aptitude, or as it is in man, so its genus is an aptitude.

II. Distinguish between an aptitude (1) inborn, or connate, (2) acquired, and (3) God-given, or divinely given. The aptitude of theology was concreate with Adam, but connate with no one. After the Fall, theologians are not born, but are made, namely taught by God through the written Word.

III. Distinguish between an acquired aptitude strictly and in the philosophic sense taken for that which is acquired through powers of nature and human industry and sagacity, and [on the other hand] an acquired aptitude in a wider meaning and theological sense [taken] for that which is acquired through the assisting grace of the Holy Spirit, through pious prayers, and through diligent reading [of] and meditation [on] Holy Scripture. Not in the former but in the latter way can theology be called an acquired aptitude.

IV. Distinguish between the acquisition itself and the manner of acquisition. The former is common to theology with other intellectual aptitudes, but the latter is truly unique in theology.

V. Distinguish between the assisting and the indwelling grace of the Holy Spirit. The aptitude of theology is bestowed not so much by the latter as by the former. For this divine information, by which theologians are made, is not precisely a work of the indwelling but of the assisting grace of the Holy Spirit, which assisting grace the unregenerate and impious also have in a certain way. But in them who are theologians both in deed and in name, that is, who are not only endowed with the theological aptitude as such, but [are] also reborn, or believers and pious, in them theology is not only from the Holy Spirit but is connected with the Holy Spirit and with His gracious indwelling.

VI. Distinguish between a ministering and a sanctifying gift of God. Theology is a gift that comes down from the Father of lights, Ja 1:5.[142] It is not a justifying or sanctifying but a ministering [gift].

VII. Distinguish between an aptitude [that is] God-given by reason of direct infusion, such as was the theology of the prophets in the Old [Testament] and of the apostles in the New Testament, and [on the other hand] an aptitude [that is] God-given by reason of invention, principle, and object, or whose principle is not human reason but the divine revelation made in the Word, whose prime purpose is not the instruction or intelligent searching and reasoning of man, but the illumination of the Holy Spirit, and whose object is not human but divine; and this aptitude is [that] of the rest of the teachers of the church.

VIII. Observe: The aptitude of theology is called God-given not because it is such through some fantastic ecstasy or enthusiasm, as the new prophets, Schwenkfelders, Weigelians, and Shakers or Quakers in England boast of their aptitude, but because it is such through a divine gift, not direct but indirect and drawn from the Word of God.

IX. Distinguish between the philosophic and natural aptitudes listed by Aristotle and the aptitude of theology, which, as being unique and supernatural, is altogether different in kind from them. And thus none of the Aristotelian aptitudes, not wisdom, knowledge, intellect, or intelligence, prudence, or art can be a kind of theology. For three theoretic or speculative aptitudes, the mind or intelligence, which is the aptitude of principles, knowledge, which is the aptitude of drawing conclusions from its principles, and wisdom, which is the aptitude of both, principles and conclusions, revolve around necessary things, knowledge of which can be attained by the genius of the human mind, without the Word of God; and the two remaining practical aptitudes, prudence, which is the active aptitude with right reason, and art, which is the effective aptitude with right reason, revolve around contingent things, some of which fall under our practice or action, others under our creation or effect, and they are in the power of man and can be arranged according to his judgment.

X. Observe: Doctrine cannot be assigned to a place of kind of theology mainly or chiefly so called, for (1) doctrine is something relative, but we are called theologians only from "theology," not relatively.[148] (2) It is an accident of theology that it can be taught and learned. But genus is of the essence of the thing defined. (3) The purpose of theologians indeed is to teach, but the purpose is outside the essence of the thing.

XI. Distinguish between theoretic aptitudes, which ultimately consist in bare contemplation of the truth, and practical [aptitudes], which indeed require knowledge of something to be done but finally neither acquiesce in it nor have it as the ultimate goal, but tend more to action and activity. We hold that theology is not to be included with the theoretic but with the practical aptitudes.

XII. Distinguish between the exercise of faith and the

exercise of godliness, or of piety. The former, namely true and living exercise of faith, is firm apprehension of the merit of Christ and of the Gospel promises; the latter is zeal for good works, which flows from the former like a stream from a spring and like fruit results from a tree. Each exercise has a place in theology, but the former, not the latter, is on our part the only means of attaining or bringing to salvation; and therefore not because of the latter but because of the former is theology called practical.

XIII. Distinguish between practical aptitudes that presuppose any kind of, or perfunctory, knowledge and practical aptitudes that presuppose accurate and thorough [knowledge]. Or distinguish between aptitudes in which knowledge is taught only incidentally and not deliberately, and the aptitudes in which knowledge is given equal high regard and is the director of practice. Of the former kind are all practical philosophic aptitudes, but the aptitude of theology is of the latter kind.

XIV. Observe: It is one thing for thought and action to be given equal high regard in theology and another to acquiesce in the knowledge, namely of God, of Christ, etc. as in the final goal. The latter is under discussion, not the former.

XV. Distinguish between the aptitude to attain [salvation] and the aptitude to bring others to salvation. Theology as such is not the aptitude to attain salvation, which is of the hearers, but [the aptitude] to bring and move others to salvation, which belongs to teachers. This bringing to salvation is true practice and activity.

Antithesis

I. Of those scholastics who hold that theology is neither theoretic nor practical, but of a higher order, likewise, affective (by some contrived third kind of aptitude, which they called affective, as Durandus

reports), because its chief purpose is to arouse the
affection of love toward God. This view is ascribed to
Aegidius Romanus and Thomas of Strasbourg.[144]

II. Of the scholastics who want theology to be purely
theoretic or speculative, e.g., Marsilius, Henry of Ghent,
and others.

III. Of the scholastics who hold that theology is a
mixed aptitude, that is, both theoretic and practical; thus
Thomas [Aquinas] holds that theology is partly a
speculative, partly a practical science. His reasoning is:
since practical science concerns things that can be done
by man, but theology concerns partly God and divine
things, which do not fall under our operation, and partly
human works, which, drawn out according to the previous
practical judgment of the intellect, are a kind of practice,
therefore in the part that deals with God and divine
things it is speculative, but in the other part, which deals
with human actions, it is practical, according to him and
his followers. But these themselves, who make theology a
mixed aptitude, are again in twofold difference. Some hold
that [theology] is simply a theoretic and in a certain
respect a practical [aptitude] or a more theoretic than
practical aptitude, e.g., Thomas, Herveus, Capreolus,[145]
[and] Cajetan, namely because it deals more especially
with divine things than with human actions. Others hold
that [theology] is more practical than theoretic, e.g.,
Bonaventura, Richard, [and] Thomas of Strasbourg.

IV. Of the papists and some Calvinists who in the
same way assert that theology is neither simply a
theoretic nor simply a practical [aptitude] but an aptitude
mixed and composite of both.

Our thesis is moreover opposed to

I. Petrus Ramus, Pareus, Sohn, Wendelin, Polanus,
Spanheim, and other Calvinists who make the genus of
theology properly so called doctrinal.

II. The scholastics, papists, and Calvinists who make
the genus of theology one of the five Aristotelian
aptitudes of the mind, namely either wisdom or

knowledge, or intelligence or prudence. And likewise [is our thesis opposed to] Musäus, who makes the genus of theology knowledge, but taken in a wider meaning for the aptitude by which, from established and unchangeable principles, we draw conclusions that are valid and of necessary truth.

III. Georg Calixtus and Horn, who define theology as an acquired aptitude. Musäus says: "Theology is indeed an aptitude connected[146] with our actions, but with elicited powers of grace and with prime truth enlightening the intellect through the revealed Word and drawing the will into consent."

IV. Georg Calixtus and Konrad Horn, who hold that theology is practical not only because of the practice of faith but also because of the zeal of good works.

Confirmation of the Thesis

We prove our thesis I. from the purpose, which is practical, and that both intermediate inward, the work—namely of a theologian—concerned about man the sinner [who is] to be converted, to be reconciled to God through faith in Christ, and to be saved, and outward, namely faith, or live exercise of faith, that is, firm grasp of the grace of God and of the merit of Christ, and final, namely bringing man to eternal salvation, and the full enjoyment and glorification of God. Now, that discipline is practical whose end is practical.

[We prove our thesis] II. from the general object. For whatever things are taught in theology, they are either directly, per se, and immediately practical or have regard to practice and are ultimately directed to it.

[We prove our thesis] III. from the special object, which is here not [that] of demonstration, such as is usual in theoretic disciplines, but that of working, namely man insofar as he is to be brought to God and [to] eternal salvation.

[We prove our thesis] IV. from the means. That discipline is altogether practical which sets forth certain means that make for the end to be introduced into the subject. Now, theology does this. Ergo. And its means are, on the part of God, the Word and the Sacraments, [and] on the part of man, faith, with a twofold action, inward or evangelical, which apprehends Christ, and outward or legal, which produces the fruit of good works.

[We prove our thesis] V. from the formal proper act. The aptitude whose formal proper act is information of the subject regarding the object, to attain the proposed end by certain means, that [aptitude] is practical. But now, the formal proper act of theology is such. Ergo. "Why cannot that aptitude be practical which is related to the restoration of man and whose unique aim is that a sinner be freed from his misery and be brought to pristine happiness?" asks Carpzov.

[We prove our thesis] VI. from the analytic process of theology. Just as otherwise all practical disciplines operate not with the synthetic but with the analytic method, which begins with knowledge of the end and moves forward from this to the subject, and thence finally to the means that make for the end. Thus also does the same order of treatment agree with theology, since it is a practical aptitude. For it does not proceed from the causes of the subject to affection to be demonstrated regarding the subject through causes, as the theoretic disciplines usually do, but rather proceeds from precognition of the end, as well of the objective (namely of God) as of the formal (namely of the full enjoyment of God or of eternal blessedness), for the sake of which all Holy Scripture was revealed, to the subject of operation (namely fallen man to be brought back to God), and the principles or causes of eternal salvation and likewise the means making for and leading to that end to be attained.

[We prove our thesis] VII. from the authority of the teachers of the church, namely the holy fathers, e.g., Ignatius, Justin, Theodoret, Gregory of Nazianzus, etc. Of some scholastics, e.g., of Scotus, who teaches that theology is per se and formally practical, not speculative, led by the argument that it is not precise because of speculation but because of practice. Of the followers of Scotus, e.g., Durandus, Aureolus,[147] Gregory of Rimini, etc. And of our more recent theologians, e.g., blessed Meisner,[148] Myslenta, blessed Gerhard, blessed Calov, Carpzov, and of others.

Sources of Rebuttals

I. Observe: When we call theology a God-given aptitude we do not mean such as is conferred on us by God directly and without all our zeal and labor, but by a God-given aptitude we mean with blessed Meisner (1) one that is opposed to aptitudes invented by human genius and zeal, (2) whose principle of knowledge is given by God, namely Holy Scripture, (3) whose object, which it sets forth, is truly divine, and (4) which is acquired not so much by our zeal and labor as by the supernatural grace of God and operation and illumination of the Holy Spirit through the Word; and so we see no reason why Musaeus says that this term is not suitable enough.

II. Observe: When they object, from Jn 17:3, that life eternal, which theology has as its intended end, consists in knowledge of God [and] that theology is therefore theoretic rather than practical, we reply by denying the line of argument, for life eternal consists in knowledge of God not as in the end but as means to the end, without which [means] no adult attains the end, namely eternal salvation and full enjoyment of God.

III. Observe: It is one thing for theology to be called, in the Scriptures and by the holy fathers, wisdom, knowledge, or prudence, in the wider and higher sense of the word, and another for wisdom, knowledge, or prudence to be properly called the genus of theology, since not every predicate is generic or definitive. As to the passages in Jb 28:28; Ps 111:10; 119:98 ff.; Pr 7:4; Ja 3¹⁴⁹:17, etc., in which the quality of wisdom is ascribed to theology, Christian theology is also called foolishness, 1 Co 1:21, 23, nevertheless this is not therefore its genus.

IV. Observe: It is one thing to speak simply of wisdom or knowledge and another to speak of wisdom or knowledge with a qualifier or restriction (spiritual, divine, hidden, etc.) expressed or understood. Likewise it is one thing to speak of wisdom and knowledge in the philosophic sense and another to speak so in the sense proper to the Holy Spirit.

V. Distinguish between a grammatic synonym and a logical genus and synonym. Spiritual, divine, hidden, etc. wisdom and knowledge are better taken as grammatic synonyms and honorary titles of theology than as its genus and logical synonyms.

VI. Observe: It is one thing for some conditions of wisdom to belong to theology and another for all to mesh with it. Certainly the chief and principal conditions of wisdom listed by Aristotle in *Ethics*, VI, do not belong to it. For it also does not belong to theology (1) to be concerned with everything: (2) to rule inferior disciplines; (3) to prove conclusions from principles; etc.

VII. Distinguish between theory and knowledge. The latter can agree with practice, in fact it is common to all intellectual aptitudes, also purely to practices, but the former forms a special aptitude contradictorily opposed to a practical aptitude. For to subsist ultimately in the contemplation of a thing, and not to subsist ultimately in the contemplation of a thing, but to be directed by its nature to practice, are differences opposed to each other in a contradictory way, which [differences] cannot combine in one and the same species. The former is the formal nature of a theoretic [aptitude], the latter of a practical aptitude. Therefore theology also lies ultimately in knowledge of the truth or it does not ultimately lie therein but tends per se to practice and activity. If the former, it is formally wholly speculative, but if the latter, it is formally wholly practical. We deny also that theology deals only with speculation about God. It has place for knowledge about God, but that [knowledge] is not speculative but practical or directed to practice.

VIII. Observe: They object that theology deals not only with worship of God but also with knowledge of God, and thus it is not only practical but also theoretic. But we deny the line of argument, for not just any kind of knowledge makes a discipline theoretic but only that which per se does not tend to practice. But now theological knowledge of God and of divine things is per se directed and tends to the exercise of faith and of piety [and] does not subsist in bare contemplation. For we know God for this reason, that we might fully and perfectly enjoy Him as our infinitely perfect and highest good both here according to the state of the present life and in the life to come.[150]

IX. Distinguish between moral philosophy and theology. In the former the end and the means are in human power but not in the latter. And from this one rightly infers that theology is not such a practical discipline as is practical philosophy. But it is false to conclude from this that theology is in no way a practical aptitude.

X. The adversaries object that if we cannot, with means, attain the purpose[151] of any kind of discipline, that [discipline] is not practical (for thus Aristotle defines a practical discipline). But now theology. Ergo. Reply: Aristotle describes not in general every practical discipline but only moral. And thus only this follows from that, that theology is not practical philosophy or such a practical aptitude as is ethic [philosophy]. And it is not valid to argue from a certain denied species to denial of the genus.

XI. Observe: The object of a practical discipline is the point of action, either in itself and its nature, or in something else which, though it be distinct from the object, is yet so connected with it that the object is recognized because of it. Thus God, though in Himself and His nature is not some action, for He is simply the first and necessary entity, yet the sanctification of His name is an action by which He that is to be known in theology is set forth.

XII. Observe: Divine things are either from God alone, e.g., the works of creation and redemption, or principally from God and secondarily and in a certain respect also from man, e.g., faith, justification, sanctification, and the whole worship of God. The former are related to points of action in the way in which God Himself [is related thereto]; but the latter are such, that is, practical, in themselves and by their nature.

XIII. Distinguish between the object of theology, which is either directly, per se, and in its nature practical, or indirectly, or that regards practice and is ultimately directed to it. The mystery of the Trinity, incarnation, [and] redemption, likewise the history of angels, devils, etc. are not indeed directly and in their nature practical or fall properly and per se under practice, yet they have not been revealed that they might subsist in knowledge of them, but that they might ultimately be directed to practice.

XIV. Observe: Knowledge of God was ordained unto worship of God and likewise [unto] practice of faith through which we aspire to life eternal, Jn 20:31: "These are written that you might believe" etc., namely that the will might worship, love, celebrate, and in true confidence embrace God the Creator and Christ the Redeemer, known by the intellect, so that man might in true faith apprehend and apply to himself the grace of God and the merit of Christ and through this faith attain life eternal and forever enjoy God. And the history of the angels and devils was not revealed simply for the sake of theory and mere contemplation, but for practice, namely that we might flee association with the latter but show ourselves worthy of their protection on this earth and of dwelling with [them] in heaven. These things should be observed over against the argumentation of Dreier, [who] says: "If theology is practical, everything in theology is practical, so that whatever belongs to theology belongs per se to practice, and thus also the knowledge of God and of the angels.

XV. Observe: In moral philosophy the knowledge by which we know the blessedness of man does not consist in honors, riches, [or] pleasures of the body nor in the quality of virtue but in action in line with virtue; likewise knowledge of the affections of the highest good, namely what is desirable because of itself, content in itself, etc., [and] knowledge of the nature of virtues and vices etc. is not formally practical, since actually and formally it is not directive of someone's activity; yet no one therefore says that ethics is in its whole self not a practical discipline but partly practical, partly speculative. For a practical aptitude, therefore, it is not required that all its acts of knowing be formally practical and actually direct some activity, but it is enough if all are per se ultimately ordained and related to practice or activity. Aristotle has this in mind when he says: "We do not ask, 'What is virtue?' in order to know but in order to become good."

XVI. Observe: The principle of theology is not infinite divine knowledge in itself (as the Jesuit Gill[152] would have it) but a kind of efflux and emanation of that divine and infinite knowledge, namely the divine revelation made in the Word. And that [revelation] is directed to action and per se intends it, since the proper end of Holy Scripture is that we believe and through faith attain life eternal, according to that [statement] in Jn 20:31: "These are written that you might believe that Jesus is the Christ, the Son of God, and that, believing, you might have life in His name." Note here that John here speaks not only of miracles narrated a little earlier but of his whole gospel, as Cyril of Alexandria, Chrysostom, Augustine, and, of more recent ones, Cornelius Jansen observe.

XVII. Let the words of blessed Meisner be noted:

"However much theologians discuss some things that seem to be merely theoretic, yet one must not therefore think that the final end itself of theology is theory or contemplation, for we do not agree to that but direct it [theology] to activity, to the attainment of salvation, or to a common end." Yet he adds thereafter that he would rather call that theological theory knowledge.

Chapter II

Of Religion, the General Object of Theology

Section I

Didactic

Thesis I

The Christian religion is the way of worshiping the true God prescribed in the Word, by which [way] man, separated from God by sin, is brought to God through faith in Christ, [who is] God and man, that he might be reunited with God and enjoy Him forever.

Note I. "Religion" is derived from *religio* [fasten, attach, fetter]. This is the derivation of Lactantius. "Bound to God by this bond of piety," he says, "we are fettered;[153] religion itself takes its name from this." And Isidore says: "It is called religion because by it we bind[154] our souls to divine worship by the bond of service."

Note II. Some religion [is] vain, other [is] pure and undefiled, Ja 1:26–27. For the word "religion" is taken either improperly and falsely or properly. It is taken improperly and falsely (1) for false religion, for example, heathen, Turkish, [and] Jewish; Georg Calixtus uses it in this sense; and yet there is only one true religion, namely the Christian. (2) For superstition or superstitious worship; thus Bellarmine calls the monastic state or the profession of the monastic order religion and defines it as the state of men who strive for Christian perfection through vows of poverty, continence, and obedience. But this religion of the papists is pure superstition, invented beyond and contrary to Holy Scripture; in fact the monastic state is clearly falsely called religion by the papists. For this word properly denotes not the state but either the norm of some state according to which God is to be worshiped, as in Acts 26:5, or the act by which God is worshiped, as in Ja 1:27. (3) In [like] manner[155] for the religious veneration of that which is not God as is [the] worship and adoration of angels, Cl 2:18, reproved and forbidden by the apostle, since such religious worship is arbitrary and voluntary worship, verse 23, and thus deceives people.

Note III. It properly means the true way of worshiping God, and that either Paradisiacal, which obtained in the state of integrity and by which man, created in the image of God, was bound to God, or Christian, which obtains after the Fall and is called Christian because we are brought to salvation alone through Christ.

Note IV. The Christian religion is taken either in a narrow sense or in a wide sense. Taken in a narrow sense it denotes first and chiefly direct divine worship, namely reverence or piety, which looks to worship of God according to the First Table of the Law; but secondly it is also taken for other works by which God is worshiped indirectly and that look to the Second Table of the Law. Love toward the neighbor presupposes love toward God, whence come secondarily, by analogy in the name of religion, the works of love toward the neighbor, in which sense the apostle James, 1:27, calls the care of widows and orphans "pure and undefiled religion before God and the Father." Taken in a wide sense, the word "religion" includes all that is taught in theology, both the things that are to be believed as well as the things that are to be done, or the things that make for piety toward God as well as for love toward the neighbor. In this sense the word "religion" seems to be taken in Acts 26:5 and Ja

1:26. On the latter passage Calov comments thus: "The word 'worship' in general designates worship of God or religion, but it should not, with Salmeron, be restricted to the worship and vows on which the religious, falsely so called in the papacy, rely."

Note V. As regards a synonym, by the Greeks religion is called religious worship in Ja 1:26, godliness in 1 Ti 4:8, reasonable service in Ro 12:1, [and] worship of God, or worship that is meet for God.

Note VI. The author or principal cause of religion is God, who, and who alone, prescribed and taught it in His Word. The ministerial cause are the prophets in the Old [Testament] and the apostles and their successors in the New Testament. Its normative principle is the written Word of God alone, since we are referred solely to it, Is 8:20. The object to be worshiped is the Triune God, Dt 6:13: "Thou shalt fear the Lord thy God, and Him only shalt thou serve."

On this passage observe: (1) The Israelites are commanded not to transfer the worship due to God alone to other or strange gods. (2) In the Hebrew the exclusive particle "only" is not added, nor is it used in Dt 10:20, where this precept is also cited, but the Septuagint translators added [it], rendering [it] thus: "and Him only shalt thou serve," which version Christ Himself approves, and He cites this statement in the same way, Mt 4:10. (3) In the passage just cited Christ appears to express that Mosaic statement in other words: "thou shalt adore the Lord thy God." But he that fears God, he also adores Him and vice versa. The universal worship due to God is understood in the generally accepted name of fear, but divine worship consists chiefly in religious adoration. Moses therefore designates universal worship, [and] Christ [designates] its chief part.

Note VII. The form of religion consists in the agreement of worship with the will of God revealed in the Word. The matter of which religion consists is faith and love toward God and the neighbor. The subject is man separated from God because of sin insofar as he is to be led back to God through Christ. The end [of religion] is reunion of people with God and the eternal enjoyment and glorification of God.

Thesis II

The properties of religion are (1) divine sublimity, (2) unity, (3) truth, (4) singularity of perfection, (5) holiness, (6) necessity, (7) usefulness, (8) age, (9) invincibility, (10) perpetuity, (11) spontaneity, (12) variety of fortune, [and] (13) energy and efficacy.

True religion enjoys (I) divine sublimity, for by origin it is divine and revealed from heaven; it is of divine revelation, not of human invention. (II) Unity; as [there is] one truth, so also [is there] one way to salvation and only one way of coming to God, Jn 14:6; Acts 10:43; 4:12; Eph 4:5–6. (III) Truth; religion is altogether true, namely in the nature of its form, which consists in agreement and conformity with the will of God revealed in the Word of truth, or because it rests solely on the Word of God, which is truth, Jn 17:17. (IV) Singularity of perfection, for it perfectly and sufficiently contains all things that are necessary for Christian faith and life. (V) Holiness, for it teaches [one] to acknowledge the holy God [and] to cultivate a holy life; it teaches holy precepts [and] reveals holy mysteries; it neither teaches false, absurd, impious, or shameful things nor commands that [they] be done. (VI) Necessity, which is self-evident[156] from the principle of obtaining salvation; if man is to be brought to God, there must be a way by which he may be brought to God. (VII) Usefulness; it leads to God, opens heaven, comforts conscience, and shows the way to true piety. (VIII) Age, for it began immediately after the fall of the first man. (IX) Invincibility; it is opposed but never succumbs, partly because of immoveable truth, which cannot be overcome, partly because of the constancy and faith of those who profess [it], whom it renders immoveable [and] invincible. (X) Perpetuity; it will never perish as long as the world exists and people remain, for it is defended against destruction by divine providence. (XI) Spontaneity; it does not want to be forced but desires to be taught, demanding free assent. (XII) Variety of fortune; it is subject to various persecutions; it is dimmed but not extinguished [and] pressed but not suppressed. (XIII) Finally energy or singular efficacy, in the glory of God to be glorified, conscience to be quieted, in people to be converted, in zeal of piety to be cultivated, in a good death to be procured, etc.

Thesis III

The sum of true religion is contained in symbols embracing the Christian faith, which are either very ancient and ecumenical, received in the whole Christian world, or more recent and, by reason of less general approval, particular.

Thesis IV

The very ancient and ecumenical symbols, or [those] received in the whole Christian world, are the Apostles', Nicene, Constantinopolitan, that of Ephesus, [and] that of Chalcedon, as also the Athanasian. The more recent symbols and, by reason of less general approval, particular and proper to the Lutheran Church are the unaltered Augsburg Confession, its Apology, the Smalcald Articles, both catechisms of Luther, and the Formula of Concord.

Note I. The ecumenical symbols are [so] called after the habitable world; taken in the wide sense, this term designates the whole inhabited world, but taken in the narrow sense, it denotes the Roman empire, as in Lk 2:1, and that not so much by reason of the instrumental cause, as though all those symbols were written by ecumenical teachers, since the jury is still out[157] regarding the Apostolic and the Nicene [Creed] as to who wrote them, and the Athanasian Creed is commonly regarded as the writing of one teacher, but (1) by reason of the object, because they are in harmony with the catholic, namely the prophetic and apostolic teaching; (2) by reason of the subject both of the receiver and of him that makes profession, namely because they have been received and approved by the catholic church of every time and place of which [time and place] they [the symbols] were born, not indeed at the same time, but successively; (3) in line with the difference of national or provincial symbols, which were composed and approved only by particular councils of nations or kingdoms or provinces.

Note II. The Apostles' Creed is [so] called not because it was composed by the apostles themselves (for otherwise it would have to be numbered with the canonical writings) but because it was composed and arranged in this order by apostolic men who heard the apostles themselves, not only from their writings but also [their] oral discourses. However, it was not taught in the church in so many words as we have [it] today but from the fourth century after the birth of Christ. Certainly up to the 400th year no form of this symbol can be shown from either the Eastern or the Western Church that agrees with both words as well as sequence and order of the articles. It is therefore a myth what Rufinus teaches in the preface of [his] exposition of the Apostles' Creed, that the apostles, about to depart from each other to preach the Gospel in the whole world, first set up for themselves, for general use, a norm of future preaching. All, therefore, seated in one place and filled with the Holy Spirit, composed this brief symbol. Augustine, in [his] second sermon for Psalm Sunday, goes farther and teaches how all the apostles individually contributed a part of the symbol. Peter said: "I believe in God the Father Almighty." John: "Creator of heaven and earth." James: "I believe in Jesus Christ," etc. But apostolic history and the apostolic epistles make no mention of this thing and ecclesiastical history is completely silent [on it].

Note III. The Nicene Creed is nothing else than a repetition of the Apostles' Creed promulgated by 318 bishops in the first ecumenical council, at Nicaea in Bithynia, assembled against Arius in the year 325 by Constantine the Great. Be it as it may regarding him who conceived [it] or him who added a pen and wrote that creed, whom some believe to have been Hosius, others Macarius, bishop of Jerusalem, [and] others Eusebius. The matter that is of greatest importance concerns the assertion of one essence of God in three persons, Father, Son, and Holy Spirit. But it labors most of all in the description of the Second Person, because at that time controversy was stirred up most of all about it. The Constantinopolitan Creed, which was composed in the year 381, is nothing else than the Nicene [Creed] repeated (hence also the ancient writers regarded both creeds as one). For "whatever is in the Nicene [Creed], that is contained in the same words in the Constantinopolitan [Creed], and whatever the Constantinopolitan [Creed] added, that is potentially or virtually in the Nicene [Creed] and was later added only for the sake of greater clarity," as Voss says. The Creed of Ephesus, which was approved in the year 431 by 230 bishops, is presented briefly in the 12 anathemas of Cyril against Nestorius. [Johann] Hülsemann does not list the [creed] of

Ephesus among the symbols but says, "What is called the creed of Ephesus are pure anathemas." The [creed of] Chalcedon was composed in the year 453 against Eutychian errors. The Athanasian Creed is believed according to the common view to have been composed by Athanasius, though Voss doubts that. Others therefore hold that it is called Athanasian not so much from Athanasius himself as author as from the teaching and faith of Athanasius. It sets forth very fully the article on God, one in essence and three in persons. But it is uncertain when and where it was composed.

Note IV. The Augsburg Confession, presented at the Diet of Augsburg in the year 1530, is, except for the Preface and Epilog, divided into two parts, the first of which sets forth faith and briefly condemns its opposites, that is, errors; and the second censures vices and errors of faith as well as of worship that have entered the Roman Church. The first part includes 21 doctrinal [articles], the second [part includes] 7 articles of abuses. And it is called unaltered, so that it might be distinguished from the Confession of Wittenberg, altered, or rather corrupted, by Philipp Melanchthon by his own and personal undertaking in the year 1540, 10 years after the confession was presented. And this corrupted [confession] is more correctly called Philippian than Augsburg Confession. For it did not see Augsburg, nor was it presented to the emperor, nor does it agree with the [confession that was] presented. And that alteration pervades all articles except the first. Especially in the 10th article was there a great change made. One should know, moreover, that this change was made to please the Calvinists and other heterodox and that only in the Latin, not in the German copy.

Note V. The Apology of the Augsburg Confession is that by which [the Confession] itself was defended, by order of the princes and states, under authorship of Philipp [Melanchthon], with the diet still in session, against the papistic confutation prepared at Augsburg (which the emperor disapproved because of the calumnies in which it abounded). This was also presented to the emperor but was not received by him but rejected. Yet this rejection by Caesar could by no means hurt the Augsburg Confession itself, but the Protestants rather defended their Confession and Apology more courageously and appealed again and again to a general council.

Note VI. The Schmalkaldic Articles were composed by blessed Luther himself in the year of Christ 1537 for this purpose, that it might be a shorter confession on hand that might be presented to a council, if there would be one. They set forth the chief points of heavenly doctrine in which there is partly agreement, partly disagreement between us and the papists.

Note VII. Each catechism of Luther, the large and the small, which Luther regarded as a precious treasure of sound doctrine, is as it were a compendium of all Holy Scripture and a brief summary outline of it.

Note VIII. The Formula of Concord is taken in two ways: (1) In general, for all the symbolical books of our church gathered into one book. (2) In particular, for the Epitome of the XI articles and their solid declaration, regarding which [articles] controversies had arisen among theologians favorably inclined to the Augsburg Confession. Briefly, it is taken either in a wide sense or in a narrow sense: in a wide sense, when [it includes] all symbolical books; in a narrow sense, so far as it includes the Epitome of the XI articles and their solid declaration. Its first formation was made in a conference at Torgau in the year 1576. Its final form [was determined 1577] at the Bergen Abbey Conference by 6 theologians: blessed Chemnitz, Jakob Andreä, Selnecker, Chytraeus, Cornerus, [and] Musculus. *The Book of Concord* was published [15]80 on June 25 (on which day 50 years earlier the Augsburg Confession had been presented to Emperor Charles V) [and] was issued "under the name of three most distinguished electoral princes, counts, barons, and orders of the empire and by a very great number of

theologians as a reminder for posterity," as Johann
Valentin Andreä has it.

Thesis V

The opposites of the Christian religion are
partly outside the church, partly within the
church: outside the church, e.g., atheism,
irreligiousness, and false religions; within the
church, e.g., superstition, hereticalness, and other
erroneous and dangerous opinions, and likewise
Epicureanism.

Note I. Atheism or irreligiousness is that which simply
worships no god at all or disparages all religion. Gisbert
Voet deals at considerable length with atheism, among
other things.

Note II. False religion is either that which worships
false gods and simply does not acknowledge the Messiah,
as ethnicism or pagan religion, or indeed appears to
worship the true God but does not worship [Him] truly
and as He revealed Himself in the Word. And though
these false and wrongly so called religions instil some
knowledge of the Messiah, yet they err egregiously both
in application, as the Jewish [religion], which does not
acknowledge Jesus of Nazareth as the Messiah and looks
for another, and in blasphemous perversion of its doctrine,
as the Turkish religion, which venerates Christ as a
prophet, yet places ahead of Him its disgraceful and
sanguinary Muhammad with the title of the last [and] so
of the highest prophet.

Note III. As false theology either teaches that false
gods should be worshiped or prescribes a false way of
worshiping the true god, so false religion is either that
which worships false gods or which does not truly
worship the true God.

Note IV. Thomas [Aquinas] defines superstition (which the Greeks call *deisidaimonia,* which word is also found Acts 25:19; more correctly its synonym is *ethelothreeskeia,* which the Vulgate also translated with "superstition," Cl 2:23) as an error contrary to religion by which [error] either unlawful worship is ascribed to God or divine worship [is ascribed to] a creature. Hence the scholastics say that superstition is committed either with regard to the object of sacred worship or with regard to the manner of worship. In fact, according to the papists, superstition includes idolatry, magic, sorceries, various kinds of divinations, etc.

Note V. Hereticalness is that which denies or corrupts partly the fundamental, partly the less fundamental articles of faith. A heretic is one who either directly and expressly or by a prone and convenient line of argument denies some article of faith necessary to be believed for salvation and who not only denies the doctrines that cannot be unknown without losing faith and salvation, but who also impugns the doctrines that indeed might be unknown without loss of salvation but cannot be denied and defends and contends for other unwholesome, pernicious, and deadly doctrines, as Augustine says.

Note VI. Some heresies are ancient, others new, or rather renewed. The better-known ancient [heresies] are Nestorianism, Eutychianism, Arianism, Photinianism, [and] Pelagianism. Of more recent heresies the better-known ones are papism, Calvinism, Anabaptism, Socinianism, Arminianism, Weigelianism, [and] Schwenkfeldianism, to which are added the errors of the antinomians, synergists, Majorists, Flacians, syncretists, etc., about which articles of faith we will write in particular in their place.

Note VII. Finally, Epicureanism is formal irreligiousness itself, by which one rejects all religion, denying the providence and vindictive justice of God, so that one does anything whatever without fear of punishment and unconcernedly.

Section II

Polemic

Question I

Was Adamitic, Abrahamitic, and Israelite, or Old Testament religion different from the Christian [religion], that is, that of the New Testament?

The Point at Issue

The question here is [1] not about religion before the Fall but about religion after the Fall; (2) not about the circumstances either of the object of religion or of the time or of the grades of clearness but about the essence itself of religion.

Thesis

With regard to essence, religion is one and the same in the Old and the New Testament.

Exposition

I. Distinguish between religion before the Fall, or that which obtained in the state of perfection, and religion insofar as it was restored after the Fall. Religion and worship after the Fall meshes, in general things, with religion and worship before the Fall (1) by reason of the source, which is divine revelation, (2) by reason of the object of worship, which is divine, (3) by reason of the mode, which is divinely prescribed, [and] (4) by reason of the purpose, which is the eternal blessedness of man. But it differs from the same in special consideration (1) by reason of principle, because before the Fall only the Law, written in the hearts as regards inward [worship], was promulgated forensically as regards outward worship; after the Fall, the Gospel also and chiefly; (2) by the reason of the object, because there God [was] beheld unveiled and in Himself, here He [is] considered in the Mediator; (3) by reason of the mode, which there consisted in works, [but] here lies in faith; (4) by reason of the purpose, namely that of blessedness, which before the Fall, as also the concrete image of God itself, was natural to man but after the Fall is supernatural to him.

II. Distinguish between essential elements and circumstantial elements. Though the religion of the Old and [that] of the New Testament is one and the same as to essence, yet some difference is granted as to circumstances, and that (1) by reason of the object of religion, with regard to the humanity of Christ the Mediator, which in the Old Testament was in types and shadows but [now] is in very substance; (2) by reason of time: then one believed in the Messiah to come, but now [in the Messiah] who has come; (3) by reason of degrees of perspicuity and clarity, which then was covered by the cloud of types and temporary things, as also of grace, which now [is] more abundant; yet religion itself is by no means to be multiplied therefore. Simeon, taking Jesus in His arms, Lk 2:28, did not change religion; a certain circumstance of faith was changed, [but] faith itself and religion remained the same, as blessed Wilhelm Leyser rightly teaches.

Antithesis

I. Of the Pelagians, who once taught that people were saved before the Law by nature, thereafter by the Law, [and] finally by Christ.

II. Of many papists, who committed the same error, holding that there was a different way of justification and so also a different [way of] salvation under the state of the natural and written law than there is now under the state of grace. Here belong those who hold that heathen can be saved without knowledge of Christ solely by the law of nature, provided they lead an honorable life.

III. Of the Socinians, who hold that God, in keeping with diversity of times, showed mankind diverse ways of worshiping Him.—In each religion of those times two things are to be seen: first, precepts or functions of piety; second, promises and threats, or at least hope of rewards and fear of punishments. The Socinians also hold that God did not require faith in Christ of the fathers who lived before the birth of Christ, nor were they saved by faith in Christ but only by obeying the divine commands. Likewise that the Jews of the Old Testament did not know the doctrine of the Trinity and the preexistence of the Son.

IV. Of the Arminians, who say that it is certain that there is no pasage from which it would be evident that faith in Jesus Christ was enjoined or was in vogue in the time of the Old Testament. Likewise, that the faith that was in the time of the Old Testament can be called indirect faith in Jesus Christ. And lest they seem to play with the word faith, they openly profess that they speak of saving [faith], by which one believes in Christ who was to die. The Arminians also did not want the Socinians anathematized for denying the most holy Trinity or even the deity of the Messiah and of the Holy Spirit, claiming that this is not a teaching of Scripture or of the church, likewise that it is not necessary and useful doctrine, believed neither in the church of the Old Testament nor in fact in the early age of the churches of the New Testament, but rather unknown and wrapped in silence. All these things really destroy the identity of the way of salvation.

V. Of the Anabaptists, Schwenkfelders, and Weigelians, who hold that only the single person of the Father was perceived and known in the Old Testament; that the mystery of the Trinity was in no way revealed to, but was hidden [from], the fathers; that the deity of Christ was unknown and thus also not worshiped in the Jewish religion; [and] that spiritual and eternal blessings were not promised to the fathers of the Old Testament (which is the same error [as that] of the Socinians and Arminians).

VI. Of the Novatians, who also cannot sincerely believe that, with regard to essence, religion in the Old Testament was one and the same as it is in the New [Testament], because they argue that the deity of Christ, as also the most holy Trinity, was not set forth to be believed by all in the Old Testament. Now, where something else and a different object to be worshiped is set forth, there a difference exists in the very essence of religion.

Confirmation of the Thesis

Our thesis is proved I. by express statements of Scripture: Acts 4:12: "Salvation is in no other; for there is no other name under heaven given to men by which we must be saved." The meaning of this statement is plain: There is one way of salvation and not many; salvation is to be sought in none other than in Christ.

Observe (1) the connection of Peter's axiom with the statement of David. With the particle "and" Peter joins these words to the statement of Ps 118:22 (which belongs to the great Hallelujah, in which the Jews by annual custom solemnly made confession of their faith) about Christ, as it were [about] the stone rejected in the crucifixion but made the head of the corner in the resurrection. (2) The clear negation, "Salvation *is not* in another" whereby every other is clearly excluded. (3) The repetition of the negation, "not in *no other*," which repetition of the negation makes the exclusion stronger. (4) The third repetition of it, "*and not*," which completely excludes another name. (5) The reason for the exclusion, "for," because another name in which there might be salvation cannot even be named; in order to make this clearly universal, the apostle adds on (6) the universality of place, "under heaven," that is, in the whole world, as [universality] of time in Lk 17:24; Acts 2:5; Cl 1:23, both of the past and of the present— [another name] is not given by which to be saved: the subjects to be saved, "among men," as many people as ever were—none had any other name of salvation. (7) The term "must be," because by reason of the divine decree one must aspire to salvation by this one way, or what thus necessarily follows, we are saved in this way and in no other.

Acts 10:43: "All prophets bear witness to Him,[158] that everyone who believes in Him receives forgiveness of sins through His name."

Observe: (1) The relative "to Him" refers to Christ, the Judge of the living and of the dead, verse 42. (2) The whole company of prophets, in fact all Scripture of the Old Testament coming in the name of prophets, comes down to this, not as simply prophesying but as witness, or not so much foretelling future things as proclaiming present things. And that it is testimony of a present thing is proved (a) by the words "receives" (not "will receive") and "believes" (not "will believe"); (b) the thing itself, namely forgiveness of sins, of which it is clear from Ps 32:1-2 and especially [from] the example of David, Ps 51:3 ff., that it was also in the Old Testament. (3) The basis of forgiveness of sins is also indicated— namely that it takes place through the name of Christ—as well as the means of application or means of receiving it on our part, namely faith—not just any [faith], but that which is in Christ and rests on His merit. And the apostle Peter clearly shows that this itself is the universal way of obtaining salvation.

Acts 15:11: "Through the grace of the Lord Jesus Christ we believe that we are saved even as they also."

Observe: (1) We are the subject of salvation, that is, the believers in the New Testament. "They also" are the fathers of the Old Testament, verse 10. (2) The manner of salvation is through the grace of the Lord Jesus Christ, by which is meant (a) the most favorable disposition of the Savior, [and] (b) the effect of that most favorable disposition, or that which, by the singular grace or love of Christ, was rendered to divine justice and is given to us, that is, His gracious and free merit, by which salvation was obtained and is to be conferred. (3) Finally there is added the means of salvation required on our part, namely faith, expressed by the term "we believe" that we are saved. We argue from the connection thus: Those who equally, like we, could not bear the yoke of the Law, they equally, like we, are saved by the grace of our Lord Jesus Christ. Now, the fathers of the Old Testament in like fashion could not bear that yoke, verse 10. Hence they are saved in like fashion as we, etc.

II. Our thesis is proved by the unity of faith in the Old and New Testament: Eph 4:5: "One Lord (or God), one faith," namely by which one comes to God. The salvation that the church of the Old Testament has in common with us presupposes a common faith with us. Paul, Ro 4, teaches at length that "Abraham was justified by faith"; moreover he teaches, verses 23 and 24, that this his faith was the same as ours; cf. Gl 3:8. Hence the argument: The faithful of all times and of all places must be saved by the same faith by which [faith] Abraham, the father of all believers, whether of the uncircumcised or of the circumcised, was saved. Now, Abraham was saved by faith in the Messiah. Ergo. Likewise: They to whom, in no other way than to Abraham, faith without works was imputed for righteousness, they are justified and saved in the very same way. Now, faith without works is imputed for righteousness, in no other way than to Abraham, to the believers both of the Old and of the New Testament. Ergo. Heb 11:26 the apostle says of Moses that by faith he esteemed the reproach of Christ greater than the treasures of Egypt. By faith in the Messiah, Moses knew the reproach of Christ, which He was to experience in the days of [His] flesh, and because he knew that to be foretold in the people of God, he wanted rather to be made part of it than to enjoy the splendor of the court and the treasures of Egypt. Therefore the object of saving faith in the Old Testament was the reproach of Christ, or whatever of reproach Christ suffered for us, taken on Himself equally from the devil and from the world, in fact also from the wrath of God, because of the sin of the world. Augustine rightly says: "The same faith in the Mediator that saves us also saved and jutified the ancients, the small with the great." The same Augustine says: "Times are different, not faith. We believe that Christ was born of a virgin, suffered in the flesh, [and] ascended into heaven; they believed that He would be born, suffer, be raised, and ascend into heaven."

Refutation

As to the passage in Acts 4:12, the Socinians object that those words are to be referred to the New

Testament (1) because Peter, not Moses or another prophet, speaks; (2) because "the salvation," because of the article, intimates a new and unheard of salvation; (3) [because] "be saved" is of the present tense; (4) because it denotes "us," Peter and the people of his age and of ages to come. Reply: To (1): Peter speaks in general terms, and that for the sake of grace in Christ, which is not to be restricted but magnified, and also using the opportunity for a prophetic statement setting forth the public confession of the church regarding this Savior. To (2): We see the article added here also to "heaven." Will therefore among the Greeks the matter be new and unheard of whenever the article is used? If "the salvation," with the article, denotes a different and new salvation, then "salvation," without the article, Heb 1:14; 5:9; Lk 1:69; Jn 4:22 [?]; 1 Ptr 1:5; etc. will denote an ancient salvation. [That is] absurd. To (3): The present tense is highly suitable to denote universality and continuity, but the past [tense], "given," has also preceded. To (4): If the present tense be strictly insisted on, also future ages are excluded; or if these are not excluded, why [are] past [ages excluded]? Surely the word "we," 2 Co 5:10, does not exclude people of a past age from judgment.

As to the passage in Acts 10:43, the Socinians object that the prophets speak of the future, not of their time, of the state of the New, not of the Old, Testament. Reply: The words of Peter are unlimited and general. All the prophets proclaimed the way of salvation through faith in Christ—[the way] to be obtained not only in the New Testament but that obtained also in the Old Testament. Let the Photinians[159] show another name by which the fathers in the Old Testament obtained forgiveness of sins.

As to the passage in Acts 15:11, the same Socinians object that the words "they also" do not denote the Fathers of the Old Testament just mentioned but heathen, that is, those converted from the Gentiles, whom the apostle calls disciples in verse 10. Also Georg Calixtus understands by "they also" those who are from the heathen. But that those words are to be referred not to the remote but to the next preceding subject, that is, not to the disciples, but to the fathers, is shown (1) by the natural arrangement of the words, in which, if it is observed, the relative word refers to the next preceding, not the remote, subject; (2) [by] the apostolic intent; for the apostles wanted to prove that man is saved alone by faith in our Lord Jesus Christ, without the works of the Law, and [they wanted to prove] that with these arguments: I. Because the Gentiles divinely received the Holy Spirit for a testimony of grace and of full reconciliation, even without a given condition of works, verse 8. II. Because God, making no difference between observers and nonobservers of works, purified the hearts of the Gentiles completely by faith, verse 9. III. Because the Law is a yoke not only grievous to be borne and not at all easy to carry, but altogether impossible to carry, and that not only by the fathers in the Old but also by us in the New Testament, verse 10. IV. Because, as to obtaining salvation and [as to] justification, nothing else can be laid on or set forth for the disciples and people of the New Testament than the grace of the Lord Jesus Christ, which was also set forth for the fathers of the Old Testament. V. If by "they also" you understand the disciples converted from heathenism to Christianity, then that which is in question is changed into the means of the terms, and one thus concludes absurdly: We believe that [we] converted Gentiles are saved just as also those converted Gentiles have been saved. VI. Those are to be understood by "they also" who can be a norm and standard according to which way the apostles and the rest of the saints might be justified. Now, the disciples cannot be the norm and standard according to which way the apostles and the rest of the saints might be justified (for the question was about their justification and salvation). On the contrary, the patriarchs and saints of the Old Testament can be the norm and standard. Ergo. Briefly, if the disciples converted from the Gentiles are denoted by the term "they also," the whole connection and line of reasoning is destroyed, since that which [is] in question is asserted in place of proof. VII. Those converted Gentiles are already included in the word "we," as is clear from verse 10. Therefore the term "they also" necessarily denotes others, and thus the fathers of the Old Testament. VIII. A contrast is set up as to the way of obtaining salvation—by fulfillment of the Law or by the grace of Jesus Christ. And the former is equally denied of all who cannot bear the yoke of the Law, and therefore the latter alone is left as regards all who want to obtain salvation. To say no more, the masculine "they also" is by a wrested construction referred by the Socinians to the very remote—and removed from it by five verses—neuter "the Gentiles" because the word "disciples" does not appeal.

Sources of Rebuttals

Observe: Christ, saying, Mt 11:12–13, "The Law and the prophets were until John, but since then the kingdom of heaven suffers violence, and the violent take it by force," does not deny that the kingdom of heaven pertained to the ancients but teaches that after John there would be a greater and more eager gathering to the church. The term "suffers violence" is explained by some passively, by some neutrally. Philipp Melanchthon explains [it] neutrally: The kingdom of God breaks out, goes forward, [and] works its way out by force; its preaching, namely, by the power of the Holy Spirit, smashes through all obstacles, not by physical but by spiritual force, tyrants and heretics notwithstanding. It succeeds by force; it cannot be hindered by the power of the devil and of the world, etc. But the sequence of the text favors the passive meaning, so that the meaning is: From the time at which John began to preach, people—who eagerly received the teaching of the Gospel and strove with great zeal for the kingdom of heaven, as if they tried to break into it by force and with some violence—were converted to Christ in multitudes and crowds.

II. Distinguish between the evangelical Old Testament and the Mosaic Old Testament; the latter does not abrogate but includes the former.[160] The same manner of justification as that of today obtained in the time of the Mosaic Old Testament, and the same manner of applying covenant blessings obtained, namely faith in Christ, but not by virtue of the Mosaic covenant but by virtue of the gracious and evangelical covenant that obtained from the Paradisaic Protevangel and always remained in force.

III. Observe: The hypothesis of the Socinians and Arminians is false, that in the Old Testament no promise of forgiveness of sins through Christ and of eternal life was known. That [hypothesis] is contradicted by clear oracles of the Old Testament, Ps 32:1; Hab 2:4; Jl 2:32, and testimonies of the New Testament, Jn 5:39; Ro 15:4; 2 Ti 3:15, which [New Testament] statements speak of the Scripture of the Old Testament and teach that it testifies of eternal life and instructs people to eternal salvation.

IV. Observe: When it is said in Gl 3:23, "Before faith came, we were kept under the Law, shut up unto future faith, which was to be revealed," by "faith" is understood either (1) the preaching of the Gospel spread by the apostles in the whole world; we grant that this [spreading] was not in the Old Testament; or (2) the clearer revelation of the grace of God made in the time of the New Testament; we likewise do not deny that comparative literal and objective clarity; or (3) the object of faith (or the faith that is believed), namely Christ, not by reason of [His] deity or of the promise of incarnation but of [His] appearance or coming into flesh, which coming of Christ into the flesh is called, with regard to the Old Testament, faith to come and to be revealed, in the passage just cited.

V. Distinguish between prescribed faith at the time of the Old Testament and exercised [faith] at that [time]. The Jews had an express command to worship and adore, not indeed another God, yet another person, besides the person of the Father, Ex 23:21 and Ps 2:7 ff. with the clear designation of the name Son. In exercised faith the Arminians mix up the faith of the weaker and [that] of the more mature as also those unhappier times, in which the Pharisees and lawyers occupied the chair of Moses, and the happier [times], in which the practice of religion was sincere and freer from the leaven of the Pharisees.

VI. In the words of 1 Ptr 1:10–12 the Socinians and Arminians stress especially the words "not unto themselves, but unto us." But we reply that those words are incorrectly wrested to exclude the prophets and the church of the Old Testament from common justifying faith in Christ with us, for that [phrase], "not unto themselves, but unto us," [is] to be explained on the basis of a comparison with the words of Paul, Heb 11:40, where the discussion is not about common salvation of souls, but about that better complement or perfection of common salvation and of faith, which was not granted them to see, they being prevented by death; but God reserved [it] for us, so that they would not be perfected without us. For God reserved the perfection of things hoped for not unto the first but unto the last times, and this [perfection] was accomplished through Christ, the Author and Finisher of our faith.

Question II

Can anyone be forced to faith and religion?

The Point at Issue

The question is (1) not about strong and effective movement or moral persuasion, but about violent and outward compulsion; (2) not about the compulsion that is effected by preaching and words, but about that which is effected by outward force and beating; (3) not about outward means by which true religion is planted and propagated, but about religion itself and faith; (4) not only about people who are outside the church, but also about those who are in the church.

Thesis

People, be they outside the church, e.g., pagans, Jews, [and] Turks, or in the church, e.g., heretics, are not be compelled by outward force to embrace the true religion and faith.

Exposition

I. Distinguish between violent compulsion and very ardent beseeching. The terms "force, compel" do not always mean the former, but sometimes the latter, as in Lk 24:29 two disciples going to Emmaus constrained Christ to turn aside to stay. Thus Jacob constrained Esau to accept gifts, Gn 33:11, that is, they earnestly constrained with insistence, beseeching, [and] pleading. Or distinguish between outward and violent compulsion and verbal, or persuasory, and argumentative motion; or, what is the same, between compulsion that takes place by power of the sword, namely by outward force against the natural inclination or will of him who is forced, and constraint that takes place by power of the word, namely by persuasory reasons by which a person is brought to agree or disagree, to will or not to will that which is advised, in the way that a doctor constrains one who is sick to take remedies; the question here is not about the latter but [about] the former [constraint].

II. Distinguish between the outward means by which religion is propagated and religion itself. A magistrate can in a certain way compel those of [his] subjects, who have been misled, to attend church often to hear the Word of God and receive other means of conversion; yet he cannot force anyone directly to religion and faith itself. The soul of people, where the seat of religion is, cannot be ruled like [their] tongues, ears, [and] feet.

III. Observe: In the matter of religion our concern is either with pagans, Turks, and Jews, who are outside the church, or with those who are in the church and enjoy the name Christian but have been infected, either truly or in the opinion of some, with some heresy; neither the latter nor the former are to be forced to true religion. For though there are differences as to lord between pagans and heretics, yet no difference is granted in consciences. For this is of divine reservations, as Stephen Báthory, king of Poland, was wont to say.

IV. Observe: It is one thing to force errorists devoted to a false religion to grasp [true] faith and another to constrain and punish those who err greatly in religion.

V. Distinguish between constraint to the true religion and constraint to false religion. It is so incongruous that a magistrate should force [his] subjects to a false religion, that he ought rather reject and uproot it; and therefore if he forces [them] to it, he sins in two things. In the same way he should not force to true religion; yet on the other hand, if he does force to it he sins less.

VI. Distinguish between violent constraint of consciences and the prohibition of public function. Though a magistrate should not force consciences to religion, yet he should not grant uncontrolled freedom to teach, profess, and practice anything whatever publicly.

Antithesis

I. Of Augustine, who, though he previously asserted in many books that no one is to be forced to a confession of faith, later claimed the authority of a slightly changed meaning of the passage in Lk 14:23, "compel [them] to come in" etc., as though those should be forced who make hedges, that is, as he himself explains, those who seek divisions in the church. Hence Estius says on this passage: "Augustine often cites this passage in order to teach that heretics are rightly compelled by punishments to enter the Catholic Church." Now, Augustine writes thus: "I said that it does not please me that schismatics are violently to be driven to Communion by force of any secular power. This indeed did then not please me because I had not yet discovered either how much evil their impunity dared or how much could be bestowed on them by diligence of discipline to change [them] for the better. This indeed follows from these words of Augustine, that he retracted [his] former view, in which he held that impunity and freedom are to be granted to heretics and that they are not to be coerced by the function of a magistrate; but he by no means held that they are to be persecuted by fire and sword. "We desire that they be corrected," he writes, "not killed; and we neither want discipline regarding them to be neglected nor do we want them coerced by the punishments of which they are worthy." And that this is what Augustine means is confirmed by Bellarmine himself. "Augustine," he says, "retracted what he once held, that heretics are not to be compelled to faith by force, and he shows at length that it is most useful, yet he always excepts the punishments of death." Etc.

II. Of the papists, who not only in theory but also in practice itself oppose our thesis and compel people with great force to the Roman-papistic religion, be they pagans or Christians, as the conversion of Indians and the Spanish Inquisition among Christians show. And *Composit. pacis Dilling.* teaches in express words: "The teaching of the Catholics is this, that it is allowed to compel the baptized to the Catholic faith by threats, prisons, and inflicted punishments." In words they indeed decree that pagans, Turks, or Jews are not to be compelled to faith. But the opposite is shown by the facts. For they wanted to force Indians to faith.

III. Of the nefarious impostor Muhammad, who was wont to say: "Moses was sent to propagate religion with threats, Christ with miracles, but he [Muhammad] with the sword." Hence Chap. 19 of the Koran has: "Kill those who are not willing to be converted."

Confirmation of the Thesis

We draw proofs for our thesis I. From the silence of Scripture: In Holy Scripture we have no command [and] no example of this coercion. For as Holy Scripture is clear and plain in other things concerning both faith and life, so that at any time we can know from it what the will of God is, it is altogether silent on this point and by being silent denies that people can or ought to be forced by outward force and arms to embrace the religion of Christ. Faith should not be commanded but persuaded, according to the [statement in] 2 Ti 4:2: "Reprove, entreat with all patience and teaching." Faith is a work of divine grace, not of human violence. "You are saved by grace through faith (certainly not of yourselves; it is the gift of God)," Eph 2:8. Faith is born not of coercion but of hearing, Ro 10:17. "We would not rule your faith," says the apostle, 2 Co 1:24.

II. From the authority of God. Religion pertains rather to the interior of the mind and the affection of hearts than [to] the outward bearing. Now, as Gregory says, God "is the king of minds and alone has dominion over consciences." Whoever therefore assumes power over the consciences of people and tries to force them to faith falsely arrogates divine power to himself. People are more easily convinced in conscience by the clear Word of God than by the frightful look of a lictor. Perhaps they are forced to pretence, but in no way to faith.

III. From the particular character of religion and of faith. Both will and religion [are] nothing, and nothing [so opposes] the reception of faith as force and violence. Hence Augustine: "Also an unwilling man is capable of other things, [but] to believe, only one who is willing."

IV. From the impossibility of effect. As the will cannot be forced by outward means, so also cannot religion. For it [religion] punishments and pain avail nothing, but they harden rather than break and persuade the spirit. Bodies can be transferred from place to place, [but] no power can be imposed on unwilling spirits.

V. From examples of the Old Testament. David, Solomon, and other Jewish kings of very different religions ruled the people, but nowhere do we read that they drove anyone by force to embrace their Jewish religion and so arrogated to themselves dominion over conscience. They were content with obedience, tributes, and taxes, which they regarded as a sign of subjection. King Nebuchadnezzar, converted to the God of Israel, did not immediately drive all provinces subject to him to the Jewish religion by outward force but caused this to be proclaimed, that it would not be allowed anyone to assail the God of Israel with blasphemy or to speak of Him disparagingly, Dn 3:29.

VI. From the decrees of ancient councils. The 4th Council of Toledo prescribed thus: "Power is not to be applied to anyone to believe, since God has mercy on whom He will have mercy and hardens whom He wants to be hardened."

VII. From the opinion of the most holy fathers. Tertullian writes thus: "It is not [the part] of religion to force religion, which ought to be engaged in voluntarily, not under pressure, since also enemies should be reasoned with from a willing spirit." Athanasius: "The Lord, not coercing but allowing personal freedom of the will, said in general to all, 'If anyone will come after Me,' and to the apostles, 'Will you also go away?'" Chrysostom adds on the same passage of John: "This is the whole force and necessity of Him who dissuades." Lactantius: "There is no need of force and injury; because religion cannot be forced, the matter should be handled by words rather than by beating,[161] so that the will might etc. Tortures and piety are far different, nor can truth be joined to force or justice with cruelty.—Religion is to be defended not by killing but by dying, not by cruelty but by patience, not by sin but by faith. If you want to defend religion with blood, with torments, or with evil, it will not be defended but defiled and violated. If the spirit is unwilling in religion, both will and religion are nothing, [and religion] is in fact taken away, actually nothing." Clement of Alexandria: "Universal religion is exhortatory and the pious worship of God." Pope Gregory writes to bishop John of Constantinople: "Your brotherhood well knows what the canons say about bishops who want to intimidate by beating. For we have been made pastors, not beaters." And the foremost preacher (Paul, 2 Ti 4:2) says: "Reprove, entreat, rebuke with all patience and teaching." These words are inserted into canon law: "But the preaching is new and unheard of that demands faith by beating." Bernard: "Faith is to be persuaded, not imposed." In Cassiodorus, the Roman king Theodoric says: "We cannot command religion, because no one is forced to believe unwillingly." And blessed Luther, who says: "To believe is something free, in fact something divine in spirit. Therefore it neither can nor should be compelled by outward force." The king of Navarre writes in letters to nobles of Aquitania: "Religion is planted in the hearts of people not by the sword but by the persuasion and by the power of teaching, and it is confirmed by the example of an honorable life." When, in the year of Christ 1555, the king of Gaul had promulgated a severe edict about extirpating the Huguenots, the senate of the Paris *parlement,* at the point of rescinding [it] from [being] an ordinance, writes among other things: "It appears fair rather to stand in the footsteps of the ancient church, which handled the matter of establishing and propagating religion not with sword and flame but with very pure doctrine and with examples of the honorable life of bishops," as [Jacques] Auguste [de] Thou reports.

Sources of Rebuttals

I. Observe: On the passage in Lk 14:23, where the Lord says to the servant, "Go out into the highways and hedges and compel (force) [them] to come in," note (1) The object to be compelled are they who are next to the hedges and fall back, that is, the pagans or Gentiles. (2) The compelling subject is the servant, by which is meant not the political magistrate but the church officer, that is, the apostles and ministers of the church, who call together the Gentiles in the highways and hedges, that is, those who live outside the true church, to that great supper which serves forgiveness of sins, reconciliation with God, the perfect righteousness of Christ, etc. (3) The act of compelling, or compulsion, is not political but ecclesiastical, that is, it is not done with outward force and compulsion but with strong and effective motivation, earnest entreaty, and moral persuasion. The Jesuit Maldonatus does not deny this, writing on Mt 22: "When he says, 'Compel [them] to come in,' he does not mean that people should be forced to faith but they are to be so entreated [and] so encouraged that they seem to be in a way compelled." This compulsion, then, which the minister of the church should bring to bear, consists in severe enlargements on the Law, threat of divine punishments, [and] exhortation to repentance. In fact, this very parable of calling together the guests to the supper rejects the meaning of compelling in regard to physical punishments. For guests were not usually compelled in that way but by importunate entreaty, constant appeal and invitation, etc. From this the statement of Lk 14 is clear, for the chief base of the adversaries, namely that in which compulsion is literally commanded, is foreign to this question, since the discussion there is about ministers of the church, not about the political magistrate; about people outside the church, but not about heretics and schismatics; not about compulsion properly [so] called, but improperly.

II. Observe: Paul uses the word "compel" in Gl 2:14, saying that Peter compelled the Gentiles to live like Jews, but he does not fault Peter for some violent compulsion by which he drove the Gentiles to embrace the Jewish faith but notes Peter's manner of life, by which he was able to attract Gentiles to Judaism. He compelled, says Augustine, "not by force of the one teaching but by the example of [his] way of life." In fact, only the attempt, not the effect, of compelling is noted. "Why do you compel Gentiles to live like Jews," that is, try to drive them to live like Jews? Compare Gl 6:12, where [the word] "compel" is explained by [the word] "desire."

III. Observe: Christ nowhere compelled people by force to embrace His teaching. He drove the merchants out of the temple with a scourge, Jn 2:16. But that was not done because of heresy. He drove them out; He did not kill them. He used a scourge and the Word, not fire and sword, as the great Prophet, not as a political prince. In fact, this was done as [something] extraordinary and miraculous. Yes indeed, when the Lord went away, the money changers returned again and were again driven out on the Day of Palms and following, Lk 19:45; Mt 21:12.

IV. Oberve: From the statement in Ro 13:4, "The magistrate does not bear the sword in vain," the papists gather that heretics, disturbers of the church and of the public peace, can not only deservedly experience the severity of ecclesiastical censure but also be punished with death by a secular judge. Reply: (1) The power of the sword is here not taken in a narrow sense in such a way that capital punishment would be specifically implied, but in a wide sense, inasmuch as it denotes every kind of punishments and vengeance, also that which is not capital, in line with the offenses. (2) Let the object be noted on which the vengeance of the sword is to be exercised. The apostle says that it is a revenger to execute wrath on him who does evil. But a heretic, as a heretic, should be prosecuted not with a physical but with the spiritual sword [and] is to be overcome with arguments, not with tortures. For faith is in the heart, where that material sword does not penetrate, but the Word of God, that two-edged sword, Heb 4:12, [does]. A physical sword cannot force consciences but [can] kill the body, Mt 10:28. But the spiritual sword kills errors, not people. But if a heretic is also manifestly a blasphemer, seditious, rebellious against the magistrate, and a disturber of the public peace, he can be restrained by prison or exile or even by capital punishment not as a simple heretic but as a blasphemer. For then that [statement] of Paul applies: "He is a revenger to execute wrath on him who does evil."

V. The adversaries cite the example of the conversion of the apostle Paul, but that act was miraculous, yet it did not lack the ordinary means of the Word. It was the work of God and not set before people as an example. A sudden light from heaven shone round about him; an elementary fire did not take him away. He fell to the ground, but he arose again. He was not pierced with a sword or treated harmfully with beating, but he could not bear the majesty of so great a Lord. Therefore we can say of Paul that, constrained, he entered in, but not that he was converted by violence.

VI. The act of Paul in Acts 13:8 ff., when he struck with blindness the false prophet who tried to turn the proconsul Sergius from the faith, was miraculous and extraordinary. But no one is allowed to try to formulate a common and general rule from miraculous deeds. Paul was an apostle, not a political prince. Paul called down blindness on Elymas, [who was] prepared by Satan to suppress heavenly truth—he did not kill him with sword or fire.

VII. Observe: It is one thing to confess with the mouth that one believes, and [it is] another thing to believe with the heart. One can be compelled to confess with the mouth that one believes, but the heart cannot be forced to believe. Those who exercise force make nothing else than hypocrites, who say one thing [but] hold something else in [their] mind.

VIII. Nor do they effect anything who cover up their deed with the example of Jehu, who killed the Baalites and slew them with the sword, 2 Ki 10:25. For the thought of the Old Testament is one thing, [that] of the New Testament [is] another. False prophets, apostates, idolaters, and seducers were at that time clearly to be killed, according to the law of the Lord, Dt 13:1 ff. But whether that forensic law should be observed so strictly in the New Testament is rightly doubted. Also, the nature of true religion is one thing, and [that] of false [religion is] another, heretics are not of one kind. Polycarp Leyser rightly says: "In the Old Testament idolaters were indeed to be severely punished, but in those laws the moral is not to be confused with the judicial. The moral is that sincerity of religion is to be preserved with the greatest zeal; this cannot be done unless we constrain him who spreads false teachings. The judicial and forensic is that capital punishment is to be inflicted on idolaters, [to] which we are not bound in the New Testament, because these political laws have ceased. But for us the statement holds: 'You do not know which spirit's sons you are. The Son of man did not come to destroy people's lives but to save,' Lk 9:55[–56]."

IX. The Jesuits are wont to set before rulers and papistic princes the examples of Constantine the Great, Theodosius, and Charlemagne, as though they propagated religion and removed heretics with a mailed fist. But the accounts show the opposite. Emperor Constantine dealt with pagans or with heretics [but] compelled neither to faith by armed force and [various] deaths, as his edicts and deeds show. Emperor Theodosius approved the punishment of exile imposed on heretics under Constantine; he did not rage against them with fire and sword but drove them out of the churches [and] prohibited those public gatherings in cities; the other punishments, which he added in order to [instill] fear, he did not carry out. Charlemagne warred against the Saxons, who defended heathen superstition tooth and nail and did not embrace the Christian faith before he gave them peace. This example is therefore foreign to the question with the papists; in fact, in their judgment Charles would not have done well if he had compelled the heathen to faith with armed force.

Question III

Can or ought a magistrate tolerate more than one Christian religion (so to say) in his area of jurisdiction?

[At that time magistrates had jurisdiction in such matters.—Ed.]

The papists simply say no. We distinguish

I. Between that which is to be desired in a Christian commonwealth and that which is to be hoped for in this life. It is to be wished for indeed, and to be incumbent on a pious magistrate to be most zealous for this, that one and the same true religion flourish everywhere, since no bond of peace and harmony is firmer than if the minds of subjects mutually agree in one and the same true religion. But full and universal agreement of that kind in this life is hardly and not even hardly to be hoped for, according to the statements in Mt 13:15; 1 Co 11:19.

II. Between the free power of a magistrate, or that which is not implicated in certain agreements or conditions, and the restricted power of a magistrate that is limited by pacts and promises or the jurisdiction of lower estates. The question concerns not the latter but the former. For sometimes a magistrate in surrender, as they call it, bound himself to tolerance of various religions and so is held to allow various religions. Hence Brochmand: "If the statutes of the realm, to which [statutes] the magistrate has taken an oath, obligate the magistrate to tolerate mixed religion, he is to stand by the promises."

III. Between tolerance of views that people hold

privately regarding true religion and allowing public practice of divergent religion. No trouble arises for the commonwealth out of the former, but the latter is pernicious for it, and freedom of public practice is not to be allowed by the magistrate to those who profess divergent religion except under pressure of extreme necessity (unless, as said, something else be promised). But let him beware lest he prohibit the proclamation of the truth, and let him not thoughtlessly apply to all what is said of individuals.

IV. Between peaceful or peaceable people of a diverse religion, and the seditious. The former can be tolerated in hope of conversion and for the sake of public peace, [but] not the latter.

V. Between a peaceful and a troubled state of the realm. When the state of the realm is peaceful and one and the same true religion flourishes in it, then the magistrate ought not receive diverse sects into his bosom. But when the state of the realm is troubled and diverse religions long already flourish and prevail in it, then the law of prudence requires that the lesser of two evils be chosen, namely that other religion be tolerated, lest the public peace be disturbed and the true church be destroyed.

VI. Note: If the heterodox are so many in number that one cannot hope to separate them from the orthodox without bloodshed, or most dangerous disturbances, or overthrow of the orthodox, it is better to tolerate the heterodox than to try something with extreme danger to the true church, the realm, and the subjects. So, when a storm has arisen, a skipper usually changes course prudently, often with changed sail setting. In gravest illnesses a doctor does not stir up putrid humors but tolerates [them], lest they build up threats to life.

VII. Note: Between violent compulsion by punishments and unlimited freedom of all kinds of religions there is room for middle ground, namely that heresies be restrained. A magistrate can tolerate heretics, but in such a way that he is concerned about their correction and conversion.

VIII. Distinguish between some indefinite kind of diversity of religion and public blasphemies and execrations of the true religion. Though at certain times any kind of diversity of religions can be tolerated by a magistrate, yet, if manifest blasphemies are added, and execrations, such as are in the synagogues of the Jews, they are to be very severely curbed and prohibited. Therefore the synagogue of the Jews is never to be allowed, since the name of Christ is blasphemed among them, Christians are cursed with portents, Talmudic fables are set forth, and the blind Jews are confirmed in their superstition. In fact, the Jews themselves are to be expelled if they do or attempt something in contempt of the Christian faith, if danger of scandal threatens the Christians because of living with them, if they are unwilling to serve Christians and show them obedience and reverence, etc. The old bon mot is well known: "Happy is the realm in which there is no Abraham (Jew), Nimrod (tyrant), and Naaman (leper), etc."

IX. Distinguish between political peace and syncretism, or a mixture of religions. A prince can decree political peace among subjects given to diverse religions, but he ought never introduce syncretism, or a mixture of religions. For such syncretism conflicts with divine commandments, both in types, Lv 19:19; Dt 22:9, and in so many words, 2 Co 6:14 ff.; Rv 3:15; destroys the unity and purity of faith, 1 Co 5:7; Eph 4:5; introduces divinely prohibited Samaritanism, 2 K 17:34, and quenches all zeal of religion and piety, so that blessed Gerhard well points out that the Holy Spirit forbade syncretism "by His own silence [and] by injunctions, both drawn up in special words and also in figures and allegories, holy portents, examples of the saints, [and] punishments." It was rejected by the church, both ancient and more recent, by creeds of confessions, namely the Augsburg [Confession] and the Formula of Concord, [and] by studies of teachers;

[it was] also condemned for reasons of arguments, as Dannhauer shows at length.

X. Distinguish between the rigid requirement of the Old Testament and the relaxation of that rigid requirement in the New Testament. In the Old Testament the church was enclosed in narrow limits. Therefore it was strictly prohibited that diversity of religion be tolerated among the people of Israel. Rather, both the false prophets were commanded to be killed and the idolatrous Gentiles to be destroyed, Dt 13:1[–5] and 7:2. But the New Testament is the time of grace, in which heretics are to be overcome with the sword of the Spirit, 2 Co 10:4, and the heavenly doctrine is to be propagated without slaying and bloodshed, Is. 11:9.

Question IV

Is the Apostles' Creed an adequate rule of doctrines necessary to be believed for salvation, so that it is a sign of inner spiritual communion and that no more things necessary for salvation ought to be demanded of any Christian?

Those who say yes [include] I. Of the scholastics, Bonaventura, Richard of Middleton, and Durandus de Sancto Porciano; especially Thomas and Dionysius the Carthusian.

II. Of the Jesuits, Gregory of Valencia, Francisco Suarez, Adam Tanner, Georg Cassander, Marco Antonio de Dominis, [and] Johann Azorius, [who] says: "It seems to me that one must say that it suffices for the salvation of each of the faithful to believe the Apostles' Creed. For this has the common belief of [papistic] theologians."

III. Of the Calvinists, John Davenant, bishop of Salisbury.

IV. Of the Novators, Georg Calixtus, Dreier, [and] Latermann. They hold, namely, that the Apostles' Creed sufficiently includes all the articles of faith, so that ignorance of others is in no way to be regarded as deleterious to salvation. And thus they make the Apostles' Creed a sign for distinguishing not only Christians from heathen, Turks, and Jews, but also the orthodox or Catholics from heretics, so that whoever receive the Apostles' Creed ought to be regarded as members of the Catholic Church and citizens of the kingdom of Christ but are by no means to be condemned as heretics, regardless of whatever errors they might hold.

Our native theologians say no, for example, blessed

Hülsemann, Calov, blessed Dannhauer, [and Johann] Musäus.

These things should be observed in deciding this question: I. it is one thing for the chief parts of Christian doctrine to be contained concisely in the Apostles' Creed, and it is another for all things that are to be believed to be set forth part by part or for all articles of faith to be set forth expressly and explicitly. It was the common view of theologians that the chief parts and sum of Christian doctrine are contained in the Apostles' Creed, of which there is no question.

II. Regarding less informed Christians and those whose minds are not infected with heterodox opinions and who have no knowledge of matters of faith besides that which we have in the Apostles' Creed, it can be granted that for them this summary is enough for salvation. But regarding others, also even the common people, namely the papists, whose minds are imbued with the opinion that they can merit the grace of God by works, that the Virgin Mary intercedes, that satisfactdion is to be rendered for temporal punishments, etc., this can in no way be granted.

III. Though in the primitive church this confession was a mark distinguishing a Christian from a pagan, yet it was not a mark distinguishing a Christian from a heretic. For the heretics themselves appealed to agreement with the Ausburg Confession.

IV. Many very necessary articles are omitted in the Apostles' Creed, namely the article on original sin, on redemption, on the personal union, on the universality of the grace of God and of the merit of Christ, on justification by faith, on the imputation of the righteousness of Christ, etc., and therefore it cannot be regarded as a sufficient and full norm of things to be believed.

V. Observe: When some of the more recent orthodox theologians praise the Apostles' Creed as a compendium containing the articles of faith, they speak of virtual inclusion, not that it explicitly and specifically presents all things to be believed.

VI. Observe: Musäus rightly says: "The Apostles' Creed contains most articles of faith at least by name or in a few words in such a way that if one did not have knowledge of the true sense from the Scriptures elsewhere or from the public teaching of the church, or add to it and supplement it therefrom, head-on conflicting heresies might easily be hidden under cover of so few words, for example, Sabellians, Arians, and Photinians ancient and more recent, Nestorians, Eutychians," etc. He lists articles necessary to be believed that are missing in the Apostles' Creed.

VII. Socinians, Remonstrants, [and] Mennonites ask nothing more than to be received and tolerated in the city of God, with only the laws and conditions of things to be believed and done expressed by the letter of the Apostles' Creed. They swear that they all hold to the Apostles' Creed according to the letter and in line with the literal sense, and they hold this one thing against us, that we require more requirements and marks of a true Christian than are stated in this creed. All pledge themselves to stand and fall by the law of the Apostles' Creed.

VIII. Here should be noted the words of Bellarmine, who says: "There is one creed, and faith is not in the words but in the meaning. We therefore do not have the same creed if we differ in the explanation. Besides, if it is enough to accept the words of the creed, scarcely any of the ancient heretics would have been justly condemned. For practically all the Arians, Novatians, Nestorians, and others accepted the words of the Apostles' Creed, but because there was disagreement in meaning, they were therefore condemned and rejected by the catholic church."

Chapter III

Of the Source of Theology

Section I

Didactic

Thesis

The source of most holy theology is divine revelation, contained in the Sacred Scriptures.

Note I. According to Thomas, the source is that from which anything, in some manner or other, proceeds. And the source is threefold: (1) of becoming, or of the thing in becoming, (2) of being, or of the thing with regard to its being, etc., [and] (3) of knowledge, on which the thing depends in knowing. In the question, "What, then, is the source of theology?" the point is not the source of being, or of the thing in becoming, but only of the source of knowledge.

Note II. The source of being differs from the source of knowledge. The source of being is that from which something has its being or on which it depends in being, and the correlate of this is the thing itself. The source of knowledge is that on which a thing depends in knowing, whose correlate is not the thing, but knowledge of the thing; the source, namely, of God's being is not given, for God does not have His being from any [source]. Yet the source of the knowledge of God, namely Holy Scripture, from which God is known, is given. So God is the source of the being and the prime cause of theology, since from

Him both the end and the means arise. But the source of the knowledge is divine revelation contained in the Holy Scriptures. One must therefore distinguish here between the One who reveals the truth, or God, and the revealed truth of Holy Scripture, prophetic and apostolic. The former is theology's source of being, for [theology] has its being from God; the latter is the source of knowledge, for theology is known and derived from Scripture.

Note III. Whatever is set forth to be known in theology is either source or theological conclusion. The only source of knowledge from which theological conclusions are drawn is the Word of God, or this: The Lord said. Theological conclusions are nothing else than truths of faith that are drawn out of and derived from the Word of God. Hence John Fisher, bishop of Rochester, says: "Scripture is as it were a kind of enclosure of all truths that are necessary for all Christians."

Note IV. The word "revelation" has two meanings and denotes either materially the revealed thing itself or formally the very act of revelation. Received in this way, it is taken either [1] broadly and in a general and rarer sense of whatever of hidden things and [things] concealed as it were under a veil have been revealed by manifestation from God, also for the things that take place through nature, as in Ro 1:19, where also those things are said to be revealed by God that can be known by guidance of the light of nature; or [2] in a narrow sense, in particular, and more usually for that special and gracious revelation made in the Word, which is called either revelation in an absolute way, or, with an addition, supernatural revelation, or revelation through the Spirit of God, Mt 11:25, 27; 16:17; 1 Co 2:10. And it is the external divine act by which God revealed Himself to mankind through His Word, that it might have saving knowledge; or, finally [3] in the narrowest sense for the revelation made to the prophets and apostles by direct illumination or direct inflowing and afflatus of the Holy

Spirit, which is primarily called revelation. But the middle meaning is [the meaning] here.

Note V. Distinguish between the source of conclusions to be known and the source of conclusions to be believed. The former is the light of nature, or right reason; the latter [is] the light of supernatural grace, or divine revelation. Thus Mt 16:17. The revelation of flesh and blood is set up over against the revelation of the heavenly Father. The former is that which nature, left to itself, without the dictation of the Holy Spirit, obtains; the latter [is that] which we have through the grace of the Holy Spirit.

Note VI. Distinguish between the source of human faith, or of opinion, which can be deceived, and divine and immoveable faith, which cannot rest on falsehood. The former is human, the latter divine belief.

Note VII. Distinguish between common sources, which many and diverse disciplines use in their proofs or for the logical inference of their conclusions, and proper [sources], which belong to a certain discipline. Here we are dealing not with common sources but with the proper and peculiar source by which a theological conclusion is established in its specific and proper being and by which it differs from the conclusions of other disciplines, and this we say is the only divine revelation traced back to the Holy Scriptures.

Note VIII. As divine revelation increased with time, so also [did] theology, [which was] based on it. And as the former so also the latter gathered up its own additions in course of time, God from time to time imparting new revelations—[additions] not indeed in the things that form the foundation of faith and of salvation (for in these things the revelation of the prime truth was always the same, and it began immediately after the Fall in the Protevangel about the Seed of the woman, who would bruise the head of the serpent, revealed by God Himself to our first parents) but in other things that make for fuller statement and understanding of these things or that concern circumstances of things, [and] rites, and ceremonies and pertain to church order and discipline.

Note IX. The source of knowledge is twofold: [1] indefinite, which is some one simple term, and [2] definite, which is some complete statement. The indefinite source of theology is Holy Scripture. But the definite source of theology, from which the doctrines of Christian faith are drawn into which they are finally resolved, is this complete statement: Whatever God has revealed in His word, or, which is the same, whatever Holy Scripture teaches, that is infallibly true and must be reverently believed and embraced.

Note X. By the word "source" is meant that which is some source, or element, from which we draw the principles of each thing, as Theophrastus says. The Holy Scriptures therefore are a certain source, and as it were the prime element from which the principles and maxims of theological conclusions are drawn.

Note XI. When therefore Holy Scriptures are called the source of theology, the word "Scriptures" is taken collectively for all prime theological truths, or inasmuch as it is a complex of many divine statements on which, as proper principles, the conclusions of faith depend and [from which] they are drawn. And thus canonical Holy Scripture is that from which, as [from] a home, the proper principles of theological conclusions are to be drawn. But the statements of Scripture are nothing else than the proper principles from which theological conclusions are drawn; for example, from that statement in 1 Jn 5:7: "There are three that bear record in heaven," etc., the mystery of the most Holy Trinity is proved as from a principle, and that theological conclusion is drawn: Therefore the Trinity of persons is given in one divine essence.

Note XII. Only the revelations once committed by the divine inspiration to writing by Moses, the prophets, and the apostles constitute the source of knowledge of theology, for no other divine revelations are surely and undoubtedly given. For after the canon of Scripture was fixed, direct revelations ceased in the church. But the old [revelations], which occurred before the birth of Christ until Malachi, the last of the prophets, up to holy men, and which were proclaimed orally by Christ himself in the days of [His] flesh, and orally and in writings after His ascension to heaven by His apostles, are so fully contained in the Scriptures recorded by Moses, the prophets, and the apostles by inspiration of the Holy Spirit, especially with regard to the things that are necessary either to believe for salvation or to do for holiness of life, that besides these no others are found.

Note XIII. When we say that Holy Scripture is the only source of theology and of theological conclusions, we have in mind not only the letter of Scripture but the meaning, both explicit and implicit, and thus also the things that are virtually contained in Scripture and are drawn therefrom by a proper line of thought. Therefore the papists, such as the Jesuits, Gonterius, Arnoldus, Franciscus Veronius, Jacobus Masenius, the Walenburg brothers, and others, have no grounds for building their new artifice as on a foundation, basis, and substructure, on this assertion of the Protestants (Holy Scripture alone is the source of faith and of theological conclusions). And their postulate is unjust which demands that we prove the doctrines of our faith solely and purely from the Word of God, apart from all interpretation and line of thought. Now, by the sole and pure Word of God they mean that which is contained in the sacred pages clearly and expressly, or in the very syllables and titles. For when the Protestants say that faith is to be proved from Scripture alone, they never meant that kind of statements of Scripture in which that which is defined may be read in so many syllables, jots, and words, nor did they through the little words "sole" [and] "only" exclude conclusions drawn from Scripture or interpretations of Scripture; but [they exclude] foreign sources or methods of knowledge that are not drawn from Scripture but from elsewhere, such as unwritten traditions, decrees of councils, definitions of popes, the authority of the Fathers, arguments of reason, new revelations, and other things, which sources are associated by the heterodox with the Word of God; we will deal with these things later in turn.

Note XIV. "To discredit the false principles regarding authority that they arrogate to themselves is the first destructive blow of those who debate. If you shall have obtained this from the pope, that Holy Scripture, contained in the canonical books, explained in its sense, not in some other [sense], [and] understood in the sources of languages, is the sole, adequate, and perfect source of faith, you will have won not only a half a victory but also a shortening of most controversies. [It was] therefore well done that at the Regensburg Conference the first and chief discussion was about he source of faith and the judge of controversies," says Dannhauer.

Section II

Polemic

The Question

Is the sole source of knowledge of theology the divine revelation contained in the Sacred Scriptures?

The Point at Issue

The question is not I. about the source of being, but of knowing; II. Not about the source of conclusions to be known, but to be believed; III. Not about the source of human, fallible faith, but of divine infallible [faith]; IV. Not about common sources, but about the proper and genuine source; V. Not about [just] any conclusions whatever, but only purely theological [conclusions]; VI. Not about revelation generally or most properly so called, but taken in a particular way, namely about that which [was] made in the Word by the singular grace of God and [is] contained in the Holy Scripture. VII. Not about Holy Scripture regarded only as to the letter, but as to meaning, both explicit and implicit.

Thesis

The sole, proper, adequate, and ordinary source of singular knowledge of sacred theology and of the whole Christian religion is the divine revelation contained in the Holy Scriptures; or, what is the same thing, canonical Holy Scripture alone is the absolute source of theology, since out of them alone are the articles of faith to be proved and deduced. But the complex source is this proposition: Whatever Holy Scripture says, that is infallibly true [and] is to be reverently believed and embraced.

Exposition

See the explanation of terms, Section I, Didactic.

Antithesis

I. Of the papists, who (1) deny that Holy Scripture is the source of faith; for thus [say] the Walenburg brothers: "Scripture is not a source that sufficiently proves faith for the faithful." And when they say that the definition of source does not fit Holy Scripture, they also consequently deny that it is the source; and (2) [who] peddle the infallibility, and decrees, and likewise the unwritten traditions of the Roman pontiff for the source of the Christian religion.

II. Of the Calvinists and Photinians, who preposterously subject the mysteries of faith to the authority of reason.

III. Of the papists and Novators, who include the consensus of the primitive church in the sources of theology.

IV. Of the Weigelians and Enthusiasts, who use private revelations and visions to prove articles of faith.

[We will speak] of all these individually in the following.

Confirmation of the Thesis

The thesis is proved I. from Scripture, which refers us to no other source than to Holy Scripture itself as the sole rule of faith, morals, and divine worship. Dt 4:2: "You shall not add to the Word, which I command you, and you shall not take away from it." Jos 23:6: "Keep all things that are written in the book of the law of Moses and turn not aside from them, neither to the right hand nor to the left." Is 8:20: "To the Law, rather, and to the Testimony; and if they speak not according to this Word, they shall not have the morning light." Lk 16:29: "They have Moses and the prophets; let them hear them."

II. [The thesis is proved] from lines of reasoning, the first of which is drawn from the sufficiency of Scripture. Holy Scripture in itself is sufficient to prove all articles of faith, and it is not necessary for either the Roman pontiff, or the consensus and authority of the church, or human reason, and private revelations and visions to be added to it.

The second [line of reasoning], from the qualities of the source. In whatever discipline, the sources ought to be prime, direct, true, infallible, sure, unquestioned, per se worthy of faith, basic knowledge, preconceded, and put beyond controversy, indemonstrable, etc. Thus also the sources of this discipline and of Christian faith ought to be prime, true, direct, indemonstrable, credible in themselves, immoveable, and unconquerable, infallible, sure, [and] unquestioned; otherwise faith could not safely rely on them. Now, all these requisites and qualities of sources belong solely and alone to Holy Scripture. And what is more, the first mark, which demands that all theological conclusions be first of all proved therefrom, agrees with Holy Scripture. Hence we know that nothing [else] can be advanced from which, as from a first principle, conclusions in theology may be properly and directly drawn. Holy Scripture is that very thing into which all theological conclusions are at length finally to be resolved. Second, it is of sure and unquestioned truth, in fact the truth itself, Jn 17:17; the word of truth, 2 Co 6:7; Eph 1:13; Ja 1:18. Indeed, since God is infallible, how can His Word be doubtful or uncertain? And third, Scripture demonstrates this its truth and authority through its own self and creates trust in its own self. Hence Nemesius: "The teaching of the divine Word of itself creates trust because it is divinely inspired." Clement of Alexandria calls the Lord's Scripture "the indemonstrable principle." Here belongs that [statement] of Bellarmine: "Nothing is better known, nothing more certain than the Holy Scriptures, which are contained in the prophetic and apostolic writings, so that he must be most foolish who denies that one must trust them."

Third, from the induction of the disciplines, of which there are in a general way two kinds, one natural, the other supernatural, [with] the former relying on human reason, the latter [on] divine authority.

Fourth, from the authority of the doctors. "We cannot speak about matters of faith on some other basis than on the basis of the Scriptures of faith," says Clement of Alexandria. "The theological sources," says Peter d'Ailly of Cambrai, "are the very truths of the sacred canon, for the final resolution of theological discussion leads to them,

and individual [theological] conclusions are in the first
place drawn from them." Alphonsus a Castro: "As in
other sciences no one who professes them denies their
first principles, so in the matter of faith, it should be
regarded as the sole and unquestioned principle by anyone
who claims to be a Christian that whatever is contained
in the sacred books is true." Hence the old custom holds,
that in the assemblies of the holy gospels the Book was
set on a high throne in the midst and source of all
Christian teachings and theological discussions, as the
Jesuit Anton von Balinghem observes.

We therefore draw the conclusion thus: Whatever
alone supplies the propositions and statements on which
theological conclusions depend in being theological
conclusions, that alone is the genuine and proper source
of theological conclusions. Now, Holy Scripture alone
supplies the propositions etc. Ergo. The major [premise]
shines by its own light. The minor is proved thus: All
conclusions are based either on the light of nature, as [on]
the formal objective reason, or on divine revelation,
likewise as [on] the formal objective reason. However, the
light of nature does not provide propositions on which
theological conclusions depend in being theological
conclusions. It therefore follows that Holy Scripture alone
is such a proper source, from which, as from a seat, such
propositions are to be drawn.

Refutation

As to the passage in Dt 4:2, observe (1) that the
discussion there is not about the Word of God delivered
by word of mouth, as Bellarmine, Cornelius a Lapide, and
others would have it, but about the written Word of
God. And thus we are referred not to the former but
solely to the latter. For Moses speaks of the Word of
God that God spoke to him; and whatever God spoke to
Moses, that Moses set down in writing and commanded

posterity to keep under the nature of Scripture and of a source of things to be believed. Ex 17:14; 24:4; Lv 11:2; Dt 31:9, 19. (2) These words were spoken not only to the Jews, as Cornelius a Lapide and Vazquez would have it, but also to Christians, since there is no reason or necessity of limitation here. Solomon also expresses this thought in a general way in Pr 30:5–6. This injunction is therefore universal, perpetual, and inviolable. It obligates also us in the New Testament, namely to adhere solely to the Word of God contained in Holy Scripture.

As to the passage in Is 8:20, observe (1): The word *Torah* in this passage does not mean only a law in particular, about not consulting soothsaying spirits and soothsayers, Dt 18:11, as Becanus would have it, but the universal law of God, or all divine revelations set down in writing; this is clear (a) from the whole context. For the prophet refers the Jews to that law, from which they had departed by idolatry, dissidence, and other sins. However, they had departed not only from that particular law, Dt 18:11, but from the whole teaching of Moses. Therefore he refers them to that in general and leads [them] to it alone; cf. Jer 31:32. (b) [It is clear] from the common name "Law." For it is the common meaning of "Law" that it is taken for the whole revealed doctrine as written, e.g., many times in Ps 119; Is 1:10; 5:24; and very often elsewhere. (c) [It is clear] from the sealing of the Law, [Is 8,] verse 16, that in verse 20 the law is meant that is said in verse 16 to be sealed [among] the disciples of the Lord. And that is the universal law of God, comprehended in Holy Scripture, as Salmeron himself admits, who tries to prove the obscurity of Holy Scripture from this passage. (d) [It is clear] from the designation "Word." In the same verse 20 the law of God is called "this Word," namely the universal written Word of God, which we ought always to follow in the things to be said in church. (e) [It is clear] from the testimony of the ancient fathers, e.g., of Origen, Cyril of Alexandria, Jerome, Basil, Haimo of Halberstadt, Nicholas of Lyra, and of others in commentary on this passage. (f) [It is clear] from the confession of the papists, e.g., of Salmeron, Gabriel, Alvaresius, Sanctius, Cornelius a Lapide, Hector Pintus, Forer, etc.

Observe (2) that the word *te'udah*, testimony, here does not mean ark of the New Testament or mercy seat, as Cornelius a Lapide, Menochio, and Tirinus would have it in commentary on this passage. For the Lord of hosts [verse 13] commands, verse 16, that the testimony is to be bound, which means a devout keeping and preservation of divine revelations as well as a perpetual observance of the divine will, but in Dt 6 this binding corresponds not to [that] of the ark, but of the book of the Law—not the response of priests and prophets regarding a future event in doubtful things, given orally, as Becanus would have it. For the word "testimony" never occurs in this sense in Scripture, and also the very particular responses of the prophets were to be tested by Scripture. But the whole doctrine, divinely revealed and comprehended in Holy Scriptures, and thus the Law and the testimony of this passage as also of Ps 19:7 [and] 78:5, are exegetically joined, and the same thing is clearly meant by those words. Also the fathers named above declare this, and some papists do not disagree, namely that "testimony" in this passage does not mean something separate from the Law but Holy Scripture itself divinely kept. This is moreover clear from the designation "Word." For what is now called Law, now testimony, is finally called "Word," namely such a Word as is now set forth to light and for the public good as the regular and unquestioned form and norm of things to be said; and that is the written Word of God. For thus [says] the Lord of hosts in an added threat: "He that speaks not according to this Word" (or this very Word, namely [that] designated by the name "Law" and "testimony," for that [term] "this" refers to the Law and the testimony), "he shall not have the morning light."

Observe (3): In this passage, lack of the morning light

is predicted in general for all, both teachers and hearers, who depart from God and His Word. For the threat strikes not only divinators, [and] not only Jews, as it pleases some interpreters, but all, and thus by its nature involves all who disregard the Word of God [and] follow false principles. By *schachar* we do not object to morning light, or light of truth, to which is opposed the darkness of errors, with Jerome on this passage; or the grace of God and the comfort and peace of the Spirit that arises therefrom, with Glassius; or the true knowledge of God and possession of eternal life, 2 Ptr 1:19, with blessed [Friedrich] Wilhelm Leyser; or finally spiritual and inner benefits, the present and indwelling grace of God and the highly efficacious concourse of all means of salvation, with Dorsche.

Observe (4): We therefore draw this axiom from this sure prophetic statement, that it is the principle and rule of faith to agree alone with the canon of Holy Scripture. For it is opposed to all other principles and means of knowing divine truth and is set forth as the full, completely perfect, and sole means and principle of knowing divine truth ordained in the church by God.

Observe (5): Though in this statement of Isaiah the exclusive [particle] "sole" [or] "only" is not added, e.g., "solely to the Law and only to the testimony" etc., yet the immediately added imprecation or threat very evidently contains the force of the exclusive [particle]. For if he that does not consult the Law and the testimony is to be sentenced to eternal darkness, it surely follows necessarily from the opposite sense that he that wants to be illumined by the light of heavenly truth should consult nothing but the Law and the testimony.

Sources of Rebuttals

I. Distinguish between the times before and [those] after Moses, or between the revelation that was made divinely to the patriarchs and was transmitted orally without the help of writing through 2,454 years, according to the calculation of Calvisius, namely from the beginning of the world until Moses, and the revelation that was set down in writing by Moses and the prophets. The former was the source of theology until Moses, the latter after Moses. For immediately after the first canon was established, which consisted of the Pentateuch, the Book of Job, and the Song of Moses, the norm and source of religion was no longer revelation transmitted orally but only that which was set down in writing. To the argument of the papists, "Whatever was a sufficient source of things to be believed until the times of Moses, that can also be a sufficient source after the time of Moses," I reply: It was sufficient for a time, therefore it is sufficient forever—that is a non sequitur.

II. Observe: It is false what the papists assert, namely Bellarmine and Becanus, that even with Scripture extant among the people of God, "the Jews used tradition more than Scripture, not only in the things that they had by tradition alone" (they meant public preaching or even private telling of parents to children) "but also in the things that were written." For, you see, people were not referred to revelations of prophets, or unwritten traditions, but to Scripture, to the Law and the testimony, Is 8:20, [and] to Moses and the prophets, Lk 16:29.

III. Distinguish between the things that are contained in Scripture [in] the very syllables and words and those that are deduced therefrom by fit, direct, and necessary consequence. Not only the former but also the latter are a source of theology and of things to be believed. For, says Nazianzus, "the things that are gathered from the Scriptures are the same as those that are written." And, as Basil says, "many things are contained in Scripture that are not contained in the letter," that is, they are contained in Holy Scriptures with regard to the sense, [but] not with regard to the letter. The Savior Himself, in a dispute with the Sadducees about the resurrection of the dead, used lines of argument, Mt 22:31.

IV. Distinguish between that which is known by its nature and in itself and that which is known to us. Holy Scripture is known by its nature, for it is revealed to all, it is clear to all, it communicates knowledge of itself to all who search it properly, even if it does not actually become known to all. "As in philosophic disciplines," says Lyra, "truth is learned by reduction to prime principles known per se. Thus truth is learned in the Scriptures taught by catholic teachers with regard to things that are held by faith, by reduction to the Scriptural canons that we have by divine revelation, in which falsehood can in no way be hidden." As to the [statement] of the papists that that which is the source ought to be known best of all; but Scripture is not known to all, Ergo,

V. Observe: Divine revelation is the first and last source of theology; advance beyond it is not allowed in theological discussion among Christians. For all doubt regarding religion is ended by divine revelation in the mind of a truly Christian person, and his faith finally so overcomes, rests, and is founded in it [divine revelation], that the mind of one who assents is freed from all fear and suspicion of deception and is made sure. Therefore papistic definition, human reason, and the direct revelation of the fanatics are false sources of faith and theology, since they do not do this.

Porisms

[For the Greeks, a porism was a proposition lying between a theorem and a problem and was directed to producing or finding what was proposed.—Ed.]

Porism I

We therefore cannot accept the fictitious infallibility of the Roman pope or his decrees and definitions as a source of our religion or of theological truths.

Exposition

Note I. The papists distinguish between the Roman pope insofar as he is considered as a private person and insofar as he is regarded as a public [person] or as pope. But he is fallible not only in the former but also in the latter respect, for his definitive statement, even cathedral pronouncement, or one as from the very chair of Peter, both can be wrong and has often been wrong.

Note II. They distinguish between the pope insofar as he is regarded personally, as a private teacher, and insofar as he is regarded judicially, as pope with the assembly of cardinals or with a general council. But he is fallible both ways.

Note III. They distinguish between premises and the

conclusion, between questions of particular fact that depend on information and testimonies of people, and decrees of faith and moral precepts to be established. Papists, e.g., Bellarmine, Stapleton, and others admit that the Roman pope can err in premises but not in a conclusion or definition itself; in questions of fact, not of law; in temporal things, but not in spiritual things; in particular things to be defined, but not in those that are set before the whole church to be believed. We say that the pope can err and has erred several times in the latter and in the former.

Note IV. The Roman pope defines something that is to be believed either beside the Word of God contained in the Holy Scriptures or according to the Word of God. If beside the Word of God, it is to be repudiated and rejected, as required by the statement in Gl 1:8. If according to the Word of God, it is therefore not believed because he defines [it] but because he follows the guidance of the divine Word—which can also be said of any other pastor or bishop. Nor will his decrees obtain the state of principle, since they themselves ought to be [but are not] derived from the Scriptures as the only source, since otherwise they cannot be regarded as true. Peter d'Ailly says: "The final resolution of theological discussion is made in line with the Scriptures, and from them theological controversies are resolved in the first place."

Antithesis

Of the papists, who make four sources of theology and faith, as [does] Bellarmine: "The written Word of God, [unwritten] traditions, the authority of the councils, and the Roman pope." But they subject the rest to the last in such a way that they really properly acknowledge only one source of theology, namely the Roman pope. Hence that [statement] is an axiom of papistic, especially

Jesuitic, theology: "Whatever the Roman pope teaches and defines, that is infallibly true." Hence Casaubon [says]: "It was established at Rome once and for all that in the matter of religion the norm of truth and right is not the Word of God, [and] not the consensus of antiquity, but of the church, that is, the infallibility of a single bishop." Alphonsus a Castro holds that "the pope is alone is to be called infallible, for this reason, that the pope is the chief part and head of the apostolic see, or of its whole aggregate, which, taken together, infallibly speaks true things in the public definition of the faith." But Jesuits refute this statement, saying here and there: "The pope indeed used the universal teachers of the church for advisers, but infallibility depends alone on this individual, not on the [great] number of advisers." And so the only, or certainly the supreme, principle of the papistic mataeology is the fictitious infallibility of the Roman pontiff. Blessed Hülsemann well says: "The principle into which the papistic faith is resolved can only be futile and uncertain by reason and judgment of the whole thing. The reason is that though they make out that they resolve their faith into Holy Scripture and prime truth according to the perceived sense of the universal church, yet they resolve the interpretation of the universal church into the interpretation of one person, who is called by them the Roman bishop."

Confirmation of the Porism

The requisites of the principle of theology do not belong to the Roman bishop or to his definition.

I. Not infallibility itself or the distinction of not erring in defining matters of faith and morals. For (a) that infallibility of the pope is a pure figment and cannot be demonstrated by any reason, no matter where it is drawn from. For though infallibility be assigned to the apostle Peter, yet it was no more hereditary than the infalliblity of the rest of the apostles, to whom, the papists agree, it was equally promised and preserved with Peter. And though the infallibility of Peter alone be hereditary, yet we deny that therefore one individual, and not rather the universal church, falls heir to it. (b) Most of the papists themselves do not grant it to the pope. Certainly the Sorbonne found the Roman bishop subject to error in matters of faith, and Bellarmine admits that the judgment of the Sorbonne is not heretical, and those who follow it are still tolerated in the church. (c) And it is not promised anywhere in the Scriptures. (d) We are nowhere commanded to accept the decrees and definitions of the Roman pope as a principle of faith. (e) The pope himself, like the rest of the teachers of the church, is bound to the rule of the divine Word. (f) He is subject to errors and has very often erred in the act itself in defining matters of faith. (g) The infallibility of the pope is in itself altogether improbable [and was] unknown to all antiquity; only in later ages [was it] set forth, timidly at first and indirectly but finally in the past century [it was] added to the rest of the errors and superstitions by the papists either to add to the heap or rashly or desperately.

II. That this principle of the papists, "Whatever the Roman bishop determines, that is infallibly true," is not valid in the first place is clear from this, that they try to prove it from elsewhere, namely from Holy Scripture itself. Mt 16:18; Jn 21:15–17.

III. We draw conclusions thus: they who (1) can err in the doctrine of faith and become heretics, (2) have decreed many erroneous doctrines officially, and (3) contradict themselves, they cannot be a source of faith and of theological conclusions. Now, Roman bishops can err and become heretics ("Since the pope is capable of all things, he is capable also of this, which is common to all, namely to err," says Alphonsus a Castro. "For he can also fall into heresy, as it is told of Pope Liberius," says Antonius of Florence), have officially decreed many erroneous doctrines (most of which could be repeated by canonical law, confirmed by papal authority, as also by the Council of Trent and by other papal assemblies), and clearly contradict themselves (Nikolas Hunnius lists 33 contradictions of officially established decrees of the Roman bishop). Ergo.

Sources of Rebuttals

I. Distinguish between personal or special prerogative and common or general prerogative. Lk 22:32: "I have prayed for you, that your faith fail not," (1) A prerogative specially obtained by Peter is designated. (2) The text does not speak of some infallibility but of final defection from faith. Christ did not pray that Peter might not fall but He prayed that he might not remain in the fall, or that the faith of Peter, who was about to fall, might not fail at the end, as He prayed a little later for the perseverance of all the apostles, Jn 17. (3) If this statement of Christ refers to the successors of Peter in the Roman see, why not to his successors in the see of Antioch—why to those rather than to these? With regard to the statement of the papists, "What is given to Peter, that is given to all his legitimate successors," the meaning of this statement, according to Bellarmine, is indeed this, that the Lord obtained two prerogatives for Peter, the one, that he himself might not ever lose the true faith, the other, that no one might ever be found in his see who would teach contrary to the true faith. However, neither meaning is drawn out of the words of Christ but [each] is read into them. The first is also false because Peter, denying Christ, lost the true faith altogether. For denial cannot coexist with faith. The second is plainly fictitious. For [there is] nothing here or anywhere else in the Scriptures about the pontificate of Peter, nothing about his see, nothing about future successors at any time in the see, [and] nothing about infallibility in the doctrine of the faith.

II. Observe: With no kind of truth do Roman bishops claim for themselves the absolute prerogative of infallibility from succession in the see of Peter, since it is not yet proved that that kind of succession was instituted by Christ in the New Testament or that Peter was bishop of Rome. In fact there is no passage of Scripture from which it might be clear that Peter was ever in Rome. And the apostles did not have fixed episcopal sees, for therein they are distinguished from bishops by the papists themselves.

III. Observe: In the statement [in] Mt 16:18, "Thou art Peter, and on this rock" etc. (on which the papists build the principle of their faith and the sum of the whole Christian matter) one must distinguish (1) between the rock, that is, Christ, who alone is the foundation of the church, or the confession of faith regarding Christ [that was] made by Peter ("Thou art the Christ, the Son of the living God"), and Peter himself. And there is by all means to be noted here (a) the variation of the name; one is *Petrus* [Peter], the other *Petra* [Rock]; the former is a proper name, the latter appellative. Christ here does not say "On this *Petrum* [Peter]" but "On this *Petram* [Rock]." (b) The condition of the predicate: That Rock is to be understood against which the gates of hell cannot prevail; but they prevailed against Peter when he denied Christ. The church is built not on Peter but on Christ alone. And it is not what one might say with Bellarmine: "Since by reason of his indefectible faith Peter is a very firm rock, it is the same: the church is built on Peter, and on the faith of Peter." For Peter is not called a rock because of the indefectibility of [his] faith, but faith and the confession of faith that Peter made regarding Christ, or Christ Himself is made the foundation of the church. (2) One must distinguish between Peter and the fictitious successors of Peter. In this passage Christ speaks of him, not of them.

IV. They object: "If in the Old Testament all were commanded, even under pain of death, to hold the decision of the high priest, Dt 17:12, with what greater right should we ascribe the same authority to the high priest of the New Testament." Thus Tirinus. Reply: It is falsely presupposed (1) that the authority of the pope in the whole Christian church is the same as that which the high priest had in the Old Testament. For that high priest was also not a type of the pope, but of Christ, who made His apostles equals. (2) [It is falsely presupposed] that the high priest at the time of the Old Testament was infallible in his judgments. The contrary is clear from various examples: of Aaron casting the golden calf, Ex 32:1; of Urijah introducing an altar of Damascus into the temple, 2 K 16:10–16; of those who condemned Jeremiah, Jer 26:8, and Christ. And, by the very confession of the adversaries, e.g., Cornelius a Lapide, and of others. (3) [It is falsely presupposed] that this judgment was [that] of the priest alone in the Old Testament, since Tirinus himself admits, on Dt 17, that there the whole supreme tribunal is spoken of that was restored by Jehoshaphat. We therefore reply on the passage in Dt 17:12: (1) It is not valid to argue from the Jewish high priest to the Roman bishop. (2) Here the authority not of one priest but of a whole great council is established, vv. 8 and 10. (3) From this the infallibility of the priest is no more built than [that] of a political judge, to resist whose judgment and authority was also fatal, v 12. (4) One was to abide by that judgment as often as it was pronounced according to the Law, otherwise not.

V. The same Tirinus objects: "The scribes and Pharisees sit on the seat of Moses, the Roman bishops sit on the seat of Christ, and whatever they say to you, observe and do, Mt 23:2." We reply: (1) These words of Christ do not speak of infallibility of the teaching of the scribes and Pharisees, since we know from the Gospel account that the scribes and Pharisees erred in many ways in the doctrine of the faith. (2) Christ teaches that they are to be heard as far and as long as they sit on the seat of Moses, i.e., continue in the teaching of Moses and do not depart from it, or insofar as they teach according to the law of Moses. (3) It is denied that the Roman bishops sit on the seat of Christ; they rather sit on the seat of pestilence, which Jerome also explains regarding doctrine. (4) We will hear the popes as long as they sit on the seat of Christ, that is, set forth His teaching. But we deservedly reject their leaven and fabrications opposed to the teaching of Christ.

VI. One must distinguish between the church itself, or the whole assembly of the faithful, embracing teachers together with hearers, and the one Teacher or also single teachers taken together. The promise of infallible assistance and guidance of the Holy Spirit, made by Christ, has for the subject "to whom" the whole church, not one teacher, namely the Roman bishop, nor the teachers taken together, or the Roman congregation itself.

Porism II

Nor is human or natural reason the source of theology and of supernatural things.

The Point at Issue

The question is I. not of reason in man before the Fall, but after the Fall. II. Not of reason as it is a subject of information but as it is or wants to be the norm and principle of proof. III. Not of organic principles but of strictly philosophic statements. IV. Not of general and transcendent but of special or particular principles. V. Not of the application of philosophic principles in mixed questions for the sake of illustration or secondary proof but by reason of decision and demonstration. VI. Not of the ministry but of the authority of reason. VII.

Not of reason considered in powers drawn from divine revelation but seen in its own powers. VIII. Not of reason corrected and enlightened from Holy Scripture but of reason unattached and left to itself. IX. Not of the enlightened judgment of reason but of the natural judgment of reason.

Exposition

I. One must distinguish between reason in man before the Fall and after the Fall. The former, as such, was never in conflict with revelation; the latter, through the fault of corruption, conflicts very often. Feuerborn rightly says: "Reason is considered either as unerring and free of sin or as a sinner. In the former, reason (in fact, the whole man) was not in conflict with God and divine things, namely before the Fall. But in the latter it is considered either in the article of sin, which it perpetrates and with its 10-foot rod measures the immense reaches of the Christian religion and thus exalts itself against the knowledge of God, or in the article of new obedience, insofar as, regenerated and renewed, it simply believes the Word of God and faithfully obeys." There reason is against God and the divine Word and, in turn, Ro 8:7 etc. But here the Word of God is not against reason, nor is this [i.e., reason] against that [i.e., the Word of God].

II. One must distinguish between passive reason, taken for the subject of information, and taken normally for the principle of proof; or between reason as it is a subject to be informed and denotes the faculty of understanding, and reason insofar as it denotes philosophy itself, or principles known from nature, and discussion or reasoning built on known principles. The former is necessary as the principle-by-which in any kind of knowledge of things, and thus also of divine [things], for man does not understand except by intellect or reason; but the latter is not admitted in the knowledge of divine things as the principle-which. Likewise must one distinguish between knowing the mysteries of faith, which is done with the intellect and reason, and that which is done by the natural light and apprehension of the intellect and of reason. Without the use of reason or of the intellect no one can engage in theology; for theology is also not to be set before brutes and animals, devoid of reason. Therefore, as man cannot taste without a tongue, so without reason, without which he is not even a human being, he cannot perceive what faith (which Augustine calls the soul of the soul) embraces in its bounds. But we deny that doctrines of faith, unknown to reason, are to be judged and deduced from principles of reason and of nature.

III. One must distinguish between reason (1) concreated with man, (2) corrupted by man, [and] (3) healed in man by grace; here we mean corrupt reason, or so far as it is considered after the Fall, in its reasonings or commentations, which it itself smashes[162] as it insists on its principles.

IV. One must distinguish between organic principles, such as are grammatic, logical, rhetorical, study of languages, etc., and philosophic principles strictly so called. The former are to be applied in theology (as aids to acquire theology),[163] since without them neither the sense nor the meaning of the words can be brought out (which [is the function] of the grammatic), nor can the figures and modes of speech be considered (which [is that] of the rhetorical), nor can connections and lines of thought be perceived nor discussions undertaken (which is [that] of the logical). Balthasar Meisner well maintains: "Who of us ever denied that one must use reason in its own way in theological matters? Or don't we use it whenever we consider either the proper meaning of the tongue or the structure of the whole context? 'Faith comes by hearing,' Ro 10:17. Now, the use of reason is required for hearing, so that a voice might be discerned and some sense be perceived. Thus we do not deny that the use of reason is necessary in confirming, in destroying, [and] in setting forth, for in all things the way and manner of teaching prescribed in the logical principles needs to be observed."

V. One must distinguish between the general or transcendental principles of reason, which hold regarding every thing, and special or particular [principles], which hold only in a certain matter, such as physical [and] mathematical. The former we allow in theology, for they are formed not only in view of finite but also of infinite nature, whence they are also called transcendental. But we deny that the latter can be applied as principles of theological conclusions, so that namely the decision and determination of these depend on those.

VI. One must distinguish between theological questions of pure faith and mixed questions (where the one term is drawn from philosophy, the other from theology). In mixed [questions] we grant that special philosophic principles can be applied, not indeed for the sake of decision and demonstration but only of illustration and of secondary proof, where the matter is defined from Scripture.

VII. One must distinguish between the ministry of reason, when it operates like the maid of a mistress or of the lady of the house (from the ancient comparison of Ambrose), and the authority of reason when it arrogates judgment to itself regarding matters unknown and set above comprehension. Mentzer [puts it] well: "Let a philosopher restrict himself within the walls of his own city and not break into the holy of holies. Let him handle what is his and not take to himself the censor's mark regarding the divine mysteries. Let him state his terms when he wants to, and let him use them in teaching in such a way that they serve matters well [and] do not rule them and make them put on a new face."

VIII. One must distinguish between reason considered in its powers that it has, acquired by its own genius [and] by its own principles, and considered in the powers that it catches from elsewhere by its net, namely from divine revelation.

IX. One must distinguish between reason unattached or left to itself or judging according to its natural principles, and reason confined within the city of the divine Word and set right, or enlightened from Holy Scripture. We do not deny that the latter can judge regarding matters of faith. But we deny that judgment regarding matters of faith belongs to the former.

X. One must distinguish between reason unbridled, or insofar as it is carried away by its reasonings, and reason bridled by the Word of God and restrained under obedience to Christ, or, in one way, by which it is in man the philosopher, as far as he is a man and a philosopher, and in another way, by which it is in man and [in] a philosopher, as far as he is a Christian and a theologian.

XI. One must distinguish between the natural judgment of reason, or what reason determines as it composes its principles and indulges in its reasonings without the bridle of superior heavenly doctrine, and judgment set right, or what reason, bridled, limited, and enlightened by the Word of God, produces.

XII. Observe: "The question here is not" (the words are those of Hülsemann) "[1] about a secondary and as it were unnecessary class of proofs when, either with truth now sufficiently proved or error sufficiently overcome, by testimonies divinely revealed, whether then it is profitable or allowed to demonstrate from the overflow the truth or error of theological teachings from the judgment of human thoughts and of inborn reason. Nor (2) is the question about the proximate instrument that on our part apprehends the true concept of divine revelation or forms knowledge in the intellect of a person who heeds the Word that is preached etc.—But the question is about the proximate principle that leads to a person's judgment, so that he decides that this statement of Scripture is to be figuratively, not literally and properly, explained. From this statement, for example, 'He ascended into heaven,' is one to gather a porism like this: 'Therefore He is not present on earth in His body'? Is agreement with connate reason sufficient principle to lead to this porism: 'The body of Christ is not seen. Therefore He [or it] is not present'?" Etc. Thus he [Hülsemann].

Antithesis

I. Of the scholastics, whose total theology is nothing else than a mixture of theology and philosophy or, by the judgment of Erasmus, a two-formed discipline put together by a kind of mixture of divine oracles and philosophic reasonings, like a kind of centaurs. For in the highest mysteries of faith the scholastics draw their conclusions from logical, physical, and metaphysical principles, with statements of Scripture disregarded or touched with a light hand.

II. Of the papists, and especially of the Jesuits, who often prove articles of faith by principles of reason. And sometimes they impugn them on basis of principles of reason. Bellarmine denies imputation of the righteousness of Christ, since it conflicts with reason. Gregory of Valencia puts this in the sixth and last place among the means of instruction for understanding Scripture and deciding matters of faith, that also natural reason be consulted.

III. Of the Calvinists, for it can be clearly shown from both their practice and [their] words that they preposterously subject the mysteries of faith to the authority of reason or even impugn them on basis of philosophic principles. Nikolaus Taurellus calls philosophy the foundation of faith. Konrad Vorst says: "The sources of faith are twofold, partly natural like sense and reason, hence all axioms [are] known by the natural light of reason, partly supernatural" etc. Goclenius writes: "I acknowledge both some ministry and [some] authority, judgment, and rule of dialectic in human wisdom and heavenly studies, that is, I hold some dialectic of teaching and understanding of both sacred and profane matters as both handmaid and mistress and judge and queen or governess." Zwingli in the Marburg Colloquy made that [statement] of Averroes and of the Socinians his own: "Nothing is to be believed that cannot be comprehended by reason, for God does not set incomprehensible things before us." Vedelius says: "Reason is a norm, not primary, but secondary, to which something of perfection might be added." But the principles of nature, which Vedelius and with him Massonius make a secondary principle of faith when they speak in theory, that they make a primary principle of faith in practice and use. Keckermann writes thus: "God wants to kindle the light of His Holy Spirit through those two clearly divine disciplines, metaphysics and logic, in the minds of people; I therefore support this use." He says further that he would make clear this mystery (of the most Holy Trinity). Peter Martyr says: "Not only the divine Word but also the words of nature are to be followed in theology."

IV. Of the Socinians, who make reason a second principle of theology, besides the Word of God, and hold that the Christian religion is to be bent according to it, since this is their axiom: "Nothing in theology is true that is not approved by reason." Likewise: "Nothing can be believed that cannot be grasped and understood by reason." The words are those of Schlichting. "What reason and common sense reject can in no way be true," says Socinus. Truly that blasphemous attack on the most Holy Trinity and the Incarnation flows from no other source than from the dictate of predominant human reason, which those people, though they do not want [it] to be seen, far prefer to the dictate of the Holy Spirit speaking in the Holy Scriptures. For thus writes Ostorodt: "If reason expressly shows that the Trinity of persons in God is false, how then would it ever, for a thoughtful person, come to mind that it is nevertheless true and can be proved from the Word of God?"

V. Of the Arminians, who grant nothing in religion unless reason agree [and] hold that judgment regarding mysteries of faith is to be entrusted to human reason, and [so] entrust [it].

VI. Of Descartes and the Cartesians; for these are his and their hypotheses: "The light of nature or the faculty of knowledge given us by God can never touch any object that may not be true insofar as it is touched by it, that is, insofar as it is clearly and distinctly perceived." Or (as he notes in the margin): "Everything that we clearly perceive is true." "From the sole reading of Scripture, perfect knowledge of not even one thing is added, nor is any clear and distinct idea acquired therefrom, nor [any] false and perverse [idea] corrected." Thus an anonymous author. But he is refuted by keener Cartesians, Wittich, Heidanus, and others strictly in profession and by Wolzogen. And Peter von Mastricht, theologian of Duisburg, has his hands full to show harmony between him and the keener Cartesians in words, hypothesis, conclusions, object, qualifications of an authentic translator, [and] in practice itself. Likewise: "Scripture needs a philosophic exposition, so that it might not be regarded as reporting falsehoods." That gave birth to these theses of theirs: (1) "Philosophy is not a handmaid to theology." See Wittich, from writings in line with Maresius, for by his example Descartes made it [philosophy] mistress. (2) "Certitude is the same whether it arises out of reason or out of Scripture." For according to the philosopher (thus they call René Descartes above others) the intellect never errs in things that are clearly and distinctly perceived.

VII. Of the Weigelians, who also make the light of nature and philosophy a source of the doctrine of faith.

Confirmation of the Porism

The thesis is proved I. By the nature of the mysteries of faith, which are set in such a way over reason that not only can they not be attained but they cannot even be perceived or comprehended, and they appear to the most learned heathen as incredible, foolish, and impossible, 1 Co 2:14; 1:20–21.

II. From the nature of reason, which is altogether blind in supernatural matters and ignorant of the mysteries of faith. Is 55:8; Mt 11:27; 16:17; Gl 4:9. It is entangled in and darkened by vanity, errors, and darkness, Ps 62:9; it is blind regarding the divine law, Eph 4:17–18; Ro 1:21–23; regarding the Gospel it is completely blind, pure darkness (and darkness cannot rightly judge regarding light and clarity), 1 Co 1:18; 2:15; Jn 1:5; Eph 5:8; and through natural corruption altogether incompetent and incapable of perceiving the mysteries of religion. 1 Co 2:14: "Natural man" (i.e., not yet regenerated) "does not comprehend" (with the comprehension of spiritual understanding, Jn 1:5) "the things that are of the Spirit of God" (the mysteries of the Christian faith, which the Holy Spirit reveals and which are not known or judged nor ought to be judged by the principles of the spirit of the world or of earthly wisdom), "for they are foolishness unto him; neither can he know [them], for they are spiritually discerned." Hence we draw the conclusion: "Whatever natural man can neither understand nor perceive when it is set before him, but regards [it] as foolishness, that cannot be discerned by his natural principles; now, natural man" (Syrus, 'the son of man, who is in the soul')," i.e., one who understands only by his own sense and ability; ergo. And one must observe here the double argument of the apostle, of which (1) one is drawn from natural opposition: "He does not perceive the things that are of the Spirit of God, for they are foolishness unto him." For man, who relies solely on the help of reason, with some natural aversion rejects the things that the Spirit of God reveals in the Word, not only as false but as foolish, i.e., completely absurd and impossible. (2) [The second is drawn] from the nature of the mysteries of faith, "for they are spiritually discerned." For the heart of the apostle's line of thought consists in this: The things that are not discerned except spiritually, that is, cannot be proved and discerned according to the thrust of the divine Word except by those who are led by the Holy Spirit, those things cannot be discerned, much less perceived or understood, by the reason of man. [Reason] is to be taken captive under the obedience of Christ and restricted in matters of faith, 2 Co 10:5. "We take captive every thought" (every thought, understanding, discernment) "to the obedience of Christ." "The mind of flesh" opposes the heavenly doctrine, Ro 8:7. "The wisdom of the flesh is enmity against God." If the very mind of our carnal reason, prone to sin, is not only opposed to God but also enmity against God and divine things, who might by his own dictate and authority judge rightly regarding God and divine things?

As to the passage in 2 Co 10:5, observe: (1) If our every thought is to be taken captive to obedience to Christ, how should it, on its own authority, judge regarding Christ and other chief parts of the Christian religion? For thus it would not be taken captive under the obedience of Christ but would be left completely free in the superior authority of its own reasonings regarding Christ. Observe (2): That the apostle speaks about the reason of the reborn (which, since our renewal ought daily to take on greater increases, Ro 7:14–15; Ph 3:9–10; 2 Co 5:2–3; Eph 4:23–24, struggles with weakness and is therefore to be taken captive) is clear (1) from the context, for reborn Paul addresses the reborn (with whom also here he numbers himself by making himself [their] partner); (2) from the term of universality, "every thought"; (3) from the nature of the matter itself, for the unregenerate are ignorant of the Gospel—hence they cannot take reason captive under its obedience.

III. From the silence of Scripture. We never read that Christ, the prophets, [or] the apostles used this principle, and Scripture never refers us to the judgment of reason in matters of faith that are to be defined. Thus also the Calvinists till now have believed with us: "What is not written is not to be believed."

IV. From the examples of the pious, who in matters of faith have not followed the judgment of reason, but while it objected in vain, believed; for example, Abraham, Ro 4:18, who "against hope" (of reason, which called for childlessness), "resorted to his hope" (of God, who promised) "that he would be the father of many nations, according to the statement" (Gn 15:5): 'So shall thy seed be.' And, not weak in faith, he did not consider in any way his own body now dead" (for begetting offspring), "for he was about a hundred years old, nor the dead womb of Sarah" (which was dead for a twofold reason, both because of age and because of sterility, Gn 16:2; 17:17), "but did not waver in distrust regarding the promise of God but was strengthened in faith, giving glory to God, informed with the certain assurance that He that promised, the same was able also to perform." Compare the example of Naaman, 2 K 5:10–11, 13; [and] of Paul, Gl 1:15–16.

V. From the example of those who, having followed the judgment of reason in matters of faith, either have erred grievously or have perished miserably; for example, the unbelieving tribune (2 K 5:12), Nicodemus (Jn 3:4, 9), Thomas (Jn 20:25), [and] the Sadducees (Mt 22:23).

Sources of Rebuttals

I. Observe: It is one thing to praise reason or the principles of reason theoretically and verbally, and [it is] another thing to apply it practically and in very deed as the principle in theological matters. The former indeed cannot be said of many scholastics, Jesuits, Calvinists, and Socinians, but the latter is common to all heterodox just mentioned.

II. Observe: It is one thing to apply philosophic principles and axioms in theology for the sake of illustration, explanation, and secondary proof where the matter is clearly defined by Scripture, and [it is] another thing to apply it for the sake of decision and proof or to acknowledge philosophic principles and reasonings formed from them as a principle in theology or to pass judgment on their basis regarding matters of faith. Those also who hold our view do the former, [but] not the latter.

III. Distinguish between [1] the organic or instrumental use of reason and its principles when they are used as instruments in the interpretation and explanation of Holy Scripture, in refuting the arguments of opponents, drawn from nature and reason, [and] in considering the meanings and constructions of words and likewise [in considering] rhetorical figures and modes of speech—and [2] the normal [use] of philosophic principles, when they are regarded as principles by which supernatural doctrines are to be tested. The former we admit, the latter we repudiate.

IV. Distinguish between the judgment of reason regarding the requirements of a good line of thought and the application of laws of a good line of thought to this or that matter or [to] judgment regarding a line of thought itself. We grant not the latter but the former to reason.

V. Distinguish between lines of thought derived from Holy Scripture by the aid of reason and conclusions drawn from the principles of nature and of reason. The former must not be confounded with the latter. For it is one thing to use (legitimate, necessary) lines of thought, and [it is] another thing to use the principles of reason. It is one thing to draw a conclusion and to put together lines of thought from statements of Scripture, according to logical rules, and [it is] another thing to draw conclusions from natural principles.

VI. Distinguish between an explicit and an implicit contradiction. The former occurs between two propositions, one of which affirms, the other denies, something; the latter occurs when in one and the same proposition the predicate contradicts the subject. The former is called contradictory opposition or also explicit contradiction; the latter [is called] contradiction in terms or implicit [contradiction]. A judgment of explicit contradiction is to be drawn altogether from the rules of connections or rather of the oppositions of logic; but human reason cannot judge regarding implicit contradiction when it does not perceive or understand the matter itself. Hence Mentzer[164] says: "In the mysteries of the Christian faith one must not regard as a contradiction whatever does not agree with human reason, but theological contradictions are to be determined by the Word of God alone. (For example: Reason, or a philosopher, through reason, from logic, can determine whether one proposition formally contradicts another. But which proposition of two in theology is true or false, that reason does not know. Thus [these] are contradictory: 'Christ is pure man; Christ is not pure man.' And both cannot be true. Only a theologian knows whether the former or the latter is true. But the nature of contradiction in terms is different. For example: 'A virgin gave birth; God is man.' A philosopher cannot know if this is a contradiction.)"

VII. Observe: Grynäus and other Calvinists charge

that we, as ungrateful people, disparage reason, which is a ray of divine wisdom. But we do not reject inborn, renewed reason, enlightened by the Word of God, held in check and taken captive under the obedience of Christ. But the latter does not take to itself judgment regarding matters of faith on its own, but draws [it] out of Scripture; it does not attack articles of faith, as [does] corrupt reason, left to itself, etc.

VIII. Observe: As to the statement in Ps 32:9, "Be not like the horse and the mule, which have no understanding," we reply: The psalmist had examined and knew the obstinate and stubborn nature of people who, against salutary reprimands (which are, as Basil attests, "healings of the soul"), "ever raise their necks like the horse and the mule," balk, and resist. Therefore he exhorts that they not want to be like those beasts but acknowledge and heed this admonition and exhortation. We are therefore enjoined by this passage to use the judgment of reason, but as assenting and conforming to the revealed Word of God. But not all that we are enjoined to use in teaching the Christian religion directly establishes judgment of Christian doctrine. For we are enjoined to use also the instrument of the ears, or hearing, etc.

IX. Observe: When we exclude the judgment of human reason from theology we do not deliver people to sophistic falsehood, brute and asinine stupidity, and anserine gullibility. But we call away from truth that leaves much to be desired to refined truth, pure and free of every spot. Nor do we make dummies and dolts of people, but we want them taught of God and instructed by the Word of God alone. We do not turn people into geese but counsel that they, with the judgment of reason curbed, form faith from its authentic principle, which is the Word of God.

X. Observe: In Ro 12:1, by "reasonable service" is not meant service that is selected from the choice of reason or is tested according to the critical judgment of reason, but here "reasonable" service is set up against the "brute" service of the Old Testament, in which sacrifices of brute animals were offered to God; now, Christians in the New Testament present themselves to God for a living sacrifice, and they offer not brute animals but their own bodies to God. (For in this passage the apostle explains "reasonable service" with the offering of our bodies, and that offering is completed not by the slaying of a living animal but by the mortification of the old man and by renewal, v. 2.) Or here the word "reasonable" denotes sincerity and is drawn not from logic but from ethics, that is, our service should be sincere and incorrupt;[165] compare 1 Ptr 2:2.

XI. Observe: As to the statement of Paul in 1 Co 10:15, "I speak to understanding people; you judge," we reply: The common sense of spiritual (for he does not mean "natural," 1 Co 2:14) man judges, but not according to principles of reason, which [reason] the apostle commands to take captive, 2 Co 10:5.

XII. Observe: (1) Christ taught reasonably, that is, He used similitudes and parable drawn from reason; yet He did not set reason up as a judge of the mysteries. A kind of illustration of heavenly matters can be drawn from things that reason supplies, but demonstration cannot be drawn therefrom, because it must proceed not from other things but from the same things. (2) The Savior indeed illustrated the mysteries with perceptible things, but He presented proof from Moses and the prophets, Lk 24:27, 44, and derived judgment from Scripture alone, Jn 5:39 and elsewhere, not from reason.

XIII. Observe: In Lk 24:25 the disciples are rebuked as fools not because they had not followed the dictate of reason (for they had done this very much) but because they had not believed the Scriptures. "O fools and slow of heart," says the Lord, "to believe in all that prophets have spoken."

XIV. Observe: Sound reason holds on reasonable grounds that heavy things sink, but if it would therefore deny that iron floats, 2 K 6:6, it would not be sound but corrupt reason, for it would oppose divine revelation.

XV. Observe: Reason is admitted as an instrument but not as a rule and judge. No one rejects the formal principles of reason; no one of sound mind accepts [its] material [principles] as a possible standard of mysteries. No material principle of reason, as such, but as it is at the same time a part of revelation, establishes faith theologically. That God is, we know from nature, [but] we believe it on the basis of Scripture alone. [This] does not follow: Axioms known by nature are sometimes part of revelation; therefore reason is the decisive standard of theological controversies.

XVI. Observe: It is one thing to forbid reason as a leader, another [to forbid it] as an attendant. Let Hagar the handmaiden serve Sarah the mistress; let reason be at hand in some certain and defined matters, in order to serve faith, not to rule [over it].

XVII. Observe: It is one thing that reason is reborn (in a Christian) and another, that, reborn, it decides and judges regarding articles of faith on the basis of the Word of God; if it does not do this, it ceases to be reborn.

XVIII. Distinguish between the true nature and the indiscipline of reason. The former is of God, the latter of the devil. There is an extremely great difference between the use, nonuse, and abuse of reason.

XIX. Distinguish between contrariety and diversity. Philosophy and the principles of reason are indeed not contrary to theology, nor [is] it to them. But those that are divinely revealed in Scripture and those that are known by the light of nature are greatly different. Therefore when the adversaries object: "Religion has many things above reason but nothing contrary [to it]," we reply: (1) The articles of faith are in themselves not contrary to reason but only above reason; but it happens by accident that they are also contrary to reason when reason takes to itself judgment regarding them on the basis of its own principles and does not follow the light of the Word but denies and attacks them. (2) The articles of faith are not only above but also contrary to corrupt and depraved reason, which holds them to be folly. Smalcius insists: "Let someone teach that one statement of Holy Scriptures conflicts with reason, and then let reason be silent in the church." We reply: When reason confines itself within its own bounds, no statement of Holy Scriptures conflicts [with it], but when reason steps out of its bounds, all mysteries of the faith oppose it, for example, that of the Trinity, of the Incarnation, etc. And though Socinians deny that these are mysteries of faith, yet that takes nothing away from the truth of the matter itself.

XX. They object: "As a dim light is not contrary to a bright one, so reason [is not contrary] to Scripture." We reply: (1) Per se there is not contrariety here, but by accident [there is]. Reason restricting itself within its sphere is not contrary to Scripture, but when it steps out of and beyond its sphere and judges by its own principles regarding the highest mysteries of faith [it is]. (2) Reason is contrary to Scripture not so far as it is a light but so far as it is blind and darkened. (3) More things are seen in a bright light than in a dim one etc. (4) Corrupt reason or its corrupt use conflicts with theology when infinite things are measured by finite things or when things are praised as universal axioms that are not such, for example, when it sets up against creation its authoritative maxim, "Nothing is made out of nothing," and against the mystery of the Trinity, "One cannot be three." For those are also not truly universals, since they cannot be verified in all individual cases. Thus "The whole is greater than its part," namely naturally, but let it remain in philosophy; yet nevertheless the parts of a whole that is blessed and miraculously enlarged can be greater than a whole that is not yet blessed, Jn 6:9, 13. Thus "The finite cannot contain the infinite," namely in physical and mathematical capacity.

XXI. Observe: The adversaries claim that they follow the lead of right reason. But one might distinguish between right reason truly and properly so called and right reason in the view of the Photinians and Calvinists. Right reason taken in the former way, namely for that which restricts itself within the limits of its object and does not arrogate to itself judgment regarding articles of faith, or that, illumined by the light of the Word, does not follow its own principles in the mysteries of faith—that does not oppose faith. But by the term "right reason" the adversaries mean that which judges regarding the mysteries of faith by its own principles. Right reason is either truly right or only conjectural. It is truly right when the Holy Spirit, through the divine Word comprehended in the books of the prophets and of the apostles, has rectified it by regeneration and illumination and it stays right insofar as and when it does not turn aside unto crooked ways, Ps 125:5, but, with the Holy Spirit, who is the right and firm Spirit, Ps 51:12, leading us in the right way, Ps 143:10, follows [His] voice and therefore does not press its own principles in deciding mysteries of faith but [follows] the statements of the Holy Spirit. But it is right only conjecturally and supposedly when, insisting on its own principles, it bends and wrests the statements of Holy Scripture to conform to them and invents various tropes and glosses.

XXII. They object: "What is true in theology is not false in philosophy, for there is one truth." We reply: (1) Truth is one in general thought, yet each discipline has its own axioms, which are not to be carried over into another frame of reference[166] but should be left in its own sphere. (2) When theology says, "A virgin gave birth," [and] philosophy [says], "It is impossible for a virgin to give birth and to remain such," they are not contrary. For theology does not say that a virgin gives birth naturally and remains such, but it says that this is done by supernatural and divine power.

XXIII. Distinguish between philosophy considered

abstractly and in the nature of its essence and philosophy considered concretely and in the nature of [its] existence in a subject corrupted by sin. In the former mode it is never opposed to divine truth (for there is no room for truth except sole and harmonious by reason of the objects in turn subject to it), but in the latter mode it is applied preposterously by a philosopher because of the ignorance of the mind and the perversion of the will, Cl 2:8.

XXIV. Theology does not condemn the use of reason, but [its] abuse and [its] affectation or directory, or [its] magisterial, normative, and decisive use in divine matters.

XXV. Observe: When Vedelius calls reason "a secondary norm of faith, to which someting of perfection might be added," Weller rightly replies (1) that it is ironwood [*sideeroxylon*] for a norm to be secondary, since a norm or canon, according to the definition of Varinus, is a true standard that in no way tolerates adding or subtracting anything. And Basil the Great may say: "An addition is for that which is lacking something, but those things (canon and rule)—if they lack something, they cannot even be properly called by those names. (2) Yet he may nevertheless maintain that reason and the principles of nature are the norm of heavenly truth, since it is valid to argue from the *est* of the third adjunct to the *est* of the second. Likewise (3) that for reason also secondarily, the first, immediate, better known, and prior things are the cause of conclusion (namely theological), which [is] absurd.

XXVI. Calvinists insist that they mean reborn reason, or human reason made spiritual after regeneration. Blessed Dannhauer replies: "This rebirth achieved something if reason is found pure in man, without afflux of residue of a sinful source till now. But the water is muddied, like water sweet—only suspect of poison, since every imagination of the human heart is evil at all times. And was not Sarah reborn? And yet she laughed at, ridiculed the promise of the Lord." Thus he [Dannhauer]. And we have shown above from the passage in 2 Co 10:5

that also reborn reason is to be taken captive under the obedience of Christ. Socinians, for example Smalcius, also protest that they speak only of reason enlightened by God. We reply: (1) Therefore reason left to itself is to be laid aside. (2) Also enlightened reason (since renewal clearly does not reach [its] zenith in this life) knows only in part, 1 Co 13:9. (3) Yet it does not know by its own powers, 2 Co 4:6, but by powers granted by grace.

XXVII. Distinguish between captive reason being renewed and rectified in this life and reason fully renewed and rectified in the life to come. The former, not yet fully rectified, renewed, and enlightened, sometimes opposes articles of faith and attacks them, if it follows its own guidance; for as the struggle between flesh and spirit remains in the reborn, so also does the struggle or conflict between faith and reason remain in them. But the latter [reason fully renewed and rectified in the life to come] excludes all opposition between faith and reason.

XXVIII. Observe in this syllogism, "A true human being has a soul and a body; Christ is a true human being; therefore Christ has a soul and a body": the major [premise] is of evident and necessary reason. The minor [premise] is of Scripture. Now, it is clear that the subject and the predicate of the question are not joined by the power and force of the major [premise] but by force of the minor [premise], in which is the conjunction of terms, which are, partly as to the sound itself, also partly at least as to force and power, the very same as the terms of the conclusion. For though a human being has a soul and body, yet the Son of God did not have a soul and a body before He began to be a human being. Therefore the cause and the principle of the conclusion is properly the minor [premise], which is of Scripture. But the major [premise] is nothing but a statement of one term, which is predicated in the minor [premise], and thus the instrument and aid for understanding the minor and for drawing the conclusion.

Porism III

And the consensus of the primitive church, or of the fathers of the first centuries after Christ, is also not a source of Christian faith, either primary or secondary, nor does it produce a divine, but only a human and probable faith.

The Point at Issue

The question is I. not regarding the principle according to man, but regarding the principle according to the truth and to the matter. II. Not regarding a principle of just any kind of theological conclusion, but of the principle simply of either theology itself and of faith, or of things to be believed. III. Not [1] regarding the Word of God in the fathers, repeated in writings, for that is and remains the Word of God, or delivered in Holy Scripture, or preached, or reduced to other written records and introduced in other books, but [2] regarding the consensus of the fathers of the first five centuries, whether it is the unquestioned Word of God and a principle of theology. IV. The question is not whether faith can be drawn from a reading of the fathers, for thus it would not be necessary to turn back to all the fathers, but faith might be had from one. V. The question is not whether that consensus of the fathers is to be praised but whether it is to be regarded as a principle of theological teachings. VI. The question is not regarding the motive of faith, which leads a person to believe, but of the very principle of faith properly speaking. And thus this is the true point at issue: Whether the consensus of the teachers of the church of the first five centuries after Christ, so far as it has thus far been able to be pointed out from their writings that have come down to us today, is to be regarded as a secondary or subordinate principle of the teaching of the faith, not only with regard to man but also with regard to the matter.

Exposition

I. Observe: By consensus of antiquity the adversaries mean consensus not in all kinds of related questions, as they say, but in articles of faith, not of all believers, nor of all teachers of the church, but only of those who lived and wrote in the first five centuries after the birth of the Savior.

II. Distinguish between the principle according to the truth, to be proved and shown simply and to the point, and the principle according to man, namely of the papists, to be refuted from that consensus, which it does not receive as a principle. The oft-mentioned[167] consensus of primeval antiquity is in every way also a principle to the matter, say the Helmstedt theologians.

III. Distinguish between the principle of the conclusion (such are all premises in a syllogism) and simply a principle. Not just any principle of any conclusion of theology is forthwith simply a principle of theology, because for a conclusion more things are also assumed than the principles simply so stated. For example, the major proposition is the principle of the conclusion also when the conclusion is theological and the major [premise] is philosophical; and yet it does not speak properly, because it says that philosophy is to be reckoned among the most assured and unquestioned principles of statements to be believed.

IV. Observe: It is one thing, that the consensus of antiquity of the first five centuries is to be praised and not to be rashly contradicted, and it is another that it is to be regarded as a secondary principle of faith.

V. Distinguish between the motive of faith or the principle of credibility, which Dorsche calls the moving principle, and the principle of faith. Among the motives of faith, or moving principles (namely those that lead people, e.g., heathen, Jews, etc., to believe), that patristic consensus regarding divine truth can be established, but it is by no means to be admitted to the rank and dignity of a principle, even secondary, such as our faith rejects, which accedes only to divine revelations.

VI. Observe: It is one thing to use that consensus as a testimony, and another to use it as a principle of faith. Our teachers also use the ancient symbols, canons of the councils, and statements of the fathers in deciding theological controversies, not as a principle but as a testimony, not infallibly to prove articles of faith thereby, but so that they might the more severely constrain the enemies who deny them.

VII. Distinguish between [1] the usefulness of this consensus in the explanation of Scripture, in the confirmation of our view, and the removal of novelty, and [2] [its] necessity for pointing out and defending the truth of the things that are to be believed.

Antithesis

I. Of the papists, e.g., of Bellarmine, Becanus, Possevino, Melchior Canus, [and] Gordon Huntley, who says: "The harmonious view of the fathers is to be regarded by all as an infallible norm of faith." Of Gregory of Valencia, [who] says: "In defining controversies of faith, also the harmonious view of all fathers or teachers ought to be regarded as a rule, because what they report regarding religion with unanimous consent is infallibly true." [And of] Sixtus of Siena, who nevertheless fills two whole books with errors of the fathers.

II. Of the crypto-papists in England, such as the Laudians, followers of William Laud, beheaded archbishop of Canterbury.

III. Of the Novators, who, following the lead of Vincent of Lerins, set up two principles of theology and of statements to be believed, one primary, Holy Scripture, the other secondary and subordinate, namely the complete consensus of the primitive church, being that of the first five centuries after Christ. Musäus says: "If the consensus of ecclesiastical antiquity, as it can be had today, is called a principle according to man, or to the matter, but secondary [and] probable, and that in the matter of certainty and authority it is subordinate to Holy Scripture and dependent on it, the term will not be unsuitable.

Confirmation of the Porism

The porism is proved I. by the nullity or nonexistence of the consensus. Many writings of the ancient teachers of the church are private [writings]. Few of those that were made public have come down to us; most have perished. Many fathers also, especially of most ancient antiquity, wrote little or nothing, and the writings of the fathers that have survived till now, they are mutilated, interpolated, and wrested. And the consensus of a few fathers is not forthwith the consensus of the whole church. The adversaries point in this direction: "Yet the best writings of the fathers have been preserved by divine providence; only the faultier ones perished." But who will make [anyone] believe this? Who will prescribe laws to divine providence? Or who will persuade [one] to confess that in the destruction of a library, whether that of Alexandria or that of Diocletian, only the faultier records perished [and] those worthy of immortality were snatched from destruction? In fact, blessed Luther rather ascribes it to divine providence that a considerable part of ecclesiastical writings perished, lest people find it necessary to devote to the contamination of the fathers and of the councils the time that should be devoted to reading and study of Holy Scripture. They insist that the consensus of the church can be sufficiently determined from the works made public. Reply: I grant that it can be particularly and probably determined, [but] I deny [it] regarding divine faith; it can in the things in which consensus appears, [but] not in others where they themselves go to pieces; it can be determined, if with one and the same consensus they agree clearly, all together, [and] persistently on some tradition of faith. Thus, for example, regarding the canon of Scripture we have a very beautiful consensus of ancient teachers if you gather all testimonies through five centuries and more; but that consensus does not appear likewise in teachings. How much disagreement [there] often [is] in writings of the fathers, also regarding the meaning of Scripture! How great a gap in times [there] often [is], how great a gap between places, where nothing is transmitted by writings! The five-century consensus would pertain only to the controversies of those times, not to heresies that arose after the fifth century.

II. By the weakness of error. Not only do the papists agree, but also the fathers themselves freely confess that the fathers were not safe from error. There is therefore great danger that one and all who are subject to error may err unanimously. In fact and in many things the fathers have actually erred, and each one of them has his own faults. Scripture alone has the distinction that it is free of all error.

III. By the multitude of spurious writings. There is hardly any of the ancient fathers into whose nest strange chickens, and they deformed, have not been put as substitutes. Many [writings under] a false name are among [them], so that it cannot up to this point be definitely established which, then, are genuine and unquestioned.

IV. By the condition and quality of that consensus. (1) A principle of knowledge, properly speaking, is contemporary at least for knowledge itself. But the consensus of fifth-century antiquity is much later than the knowledge itself of divine things. (2) A principle is at least of the same authority as is the knowledge itself and the teachings to be proved therefrom. But now the consensus of antiquity is not of the authority of which are articles of faith. For we believe these by divine faith, [but] that by human faith. For the fathers, either all or most of them, even though they agree on some matter, or even mutually, in testifying, defining, [or] interpreting, yet do not ever engender divine faith, but only human [faith], which stands over against the fear that it rests on a false base and [is] thus probable and historical. The consensus of antiquity is moreover confused, imperfect, comparable with difficulty, and leads us into many doubts. That way of speaking, "The consensus of antiquity is a principle of teachings of the faith," is (1) new, (2) false, (3) absurd, (4) unknown to antiquity, (5) rejected by most of us, [and] (6) rests on no divine authorities.

V. By the denial of the requisites of a principle. The requisites of a principle properly so called do not fit that patristic consensus: (I) Not infallibility, both because the individual fathers were human beings who could deceive and be deceived and because the infalliblity of things taken together cannot be shown either a priori, that is, from the nature of the matter, or a posteriori, or from some divine promise, in such a way that if they are not infallible in themselves, they might be such because of a special promise of God. But such a promise was not recorded [in] any divine writings. "If the individual fathers" (the words are those of Dannhauer) "[were] born and subject to the danger of hallucination at a time when it was common to err, by what special power [would] all [be] protected [against error], especially with causes of errors posited, such as ignorance of languages, especially of Hebrew, carelessness in following [someone's lead], commixture of profane philosophy," etc. Dannhauer cites examples of universal consensus in error. (II) Not invariability. The writings of the fathers are not self-consistent. The fathers often disagree with each other. They often contradict each other. They also sometimes speak with more assurance before strifes arose. (III) Not universality, for that consensus cannot be found at every time and at all places. (IV) Not priority, for it is later than the teachings of the faith themselves.

VI. By the argument of the absurd. That fifth-century consensus is a principle either because it rightly draws from the Holy Scriptures the things that are to be believed or because it faithfully and infallibly preserves the memory of the apostolic assemblies and traditions. If the latter, the way is now open for the papists to an unwritten Word of God. If the former, there will now be as many principles as centuries, rather as many times, in which the things to be believed were rightly drawn from Holy Scriptures; but that is incongruous and absurd.

Sources of Rebuttals

I. Observe: The adversaries stress the promise of Christ in Mt 28:20, "I am with you" etc. But how will they prove [this] from that gracious divine presence with the church, which the Savior there promised would continue, namely that the testimonies of the teachers of the church or of those who agree with the fathers would have the part of a secondary or subordinate principle? We know the promised presence of the Lord Jesus from those words; but we indeed do not gather that effect of the presence from any unquestioned principle and testimony.

II. Observe: It is one thing to be a norm and rule of things to be believed absolutely, and [it is] another thing to be a norm and rule in a certain respect and as it were with certain limits. Confessions and bodies of doctrine, e.g., the Augsburg Confession, Corpus Julium, Prutenicum, Formula of Concord, etc., are norm and rule not without reservation but in a certain respect, a symbol[168] norm, testimonial of the public doctrine of some particular churches. But its principle and norm is Holy Scripture, from which the authors of those confessions draw that which they themselves believed was to be believed and what they wanted to be believed in their territories.

III. The adversaries emphasize that statement of Paul in 1 Ti 3:15: "The church of the living God is the pillar and mainstay of the truth." But (1) it is one thing to be the pillar and mainstay of the truth, and another to be some subordinate principle of the truth. In the passage cited, the church is called the pillar and mainstay of the truth through Scripture, but not by means of an infallible proponent, which the papists want, or of some subordinate principle, which the Novators want. (2) In the place of the subject he puts the whole assembly of the faithful, not only the teachers, much less does he give only the writers of the primitive church to the distinction of infallibility, which writers are here in question. Therefore the axiom belonging to the whole aggregate taken collectively is falsely restricted to only the class of extant writers.

IV. Observe: It is one thing to be the pillar and mainstay of the truth absolutely and first, and another to be the pillar and mainstay of the truth according to something, or with a certain limitation. The church is the pillar and mainstay of the truth not in the former but in the latter way, namely so far as it itself rests on the heavenly truth contained in Holy Scripture as foundation. It is called the pillar and mainstay of the truth not because it sustains the truth in an active sense, but because it is sustained by the truth, according to Cornelius a Lapide. The church is passively established in faith and the truth by the assistance of the Holy Spirit.

V. Distinguish between the honor due to the teachers of the ancient church because of the antiquity, diligence, and labors endured, and their infallibility in teaching and testifying. In that way are the ancient fathers to be honored, lest the divine honor of mother Scripture be vitiated.

VI. Observe: If that patristic consensus or consensus of the primitive church is itself the genuine sense of Holy Scripture or, as Horn says, "the vigor and strength[169] of Scripture (*der rechte Safft und Krafft der Schrifft*)," it is therefore not some subordinate and secondary principle but the very highest and credible-in-itself principle, set forth by the ministry of the church and applied for determining certain cases—unless one wants to say absurdly that Holy Scripture is the primary principle of theology, but that its genuine sense, or the very vigor and strength, as it were, of Scripture, contained in writings of the fathers, is a secondary principle.

VII. They object: A principle is that whence something is or is known; now, theological conclusions are known and proved from the writings of the fathers; ergo. We reply: Theological conclusions are indeed proved thence, but not in such a way that Christian faith undoubtedly rests on them. One must therefore distinguish [among] proofs of a topic those that result in some verisimilitude or probability and [those that are] infallible and apodictic proofs, on which our faith can and should rest.

VIII. Observe: The question is regarding the principle of faith and of things to be believed, not of just any kind of principle of theological conclusions. Though the testimonies of the fathers can in their own way be called a principle of any kind of theological conclusions, namely insofar as this or that in theology is proved from them, yet we deny that they are a principle of divine faith and of the very things to be believed. For the principle of divine faith is not a human word but only the Word of God. The principle of a syllogism is not always the principle in the matter itself. Motives of faith also generate conclusions, and yet they are not properly called principles of faith.

IX. Latermann stresses the promise in Mt 16:18 as to the portals of hell not to prevail against the church. But (1) the portals of hell (heresies and persecutions sent against the church by the devil) often prevailed against the writers of the church also of the first centuries. (2) The point of this statement is not regarding the teachers taken separately from the rest of the Christian people, with whom this question deals, much less regarding the smallest particles of those who enjoined something in writing.

X. Latermann emphasizes that the saints who overcame that great dragon by the blood of the Lamb and by the Word of His testimony (while they fearlessly spoke the testimony of the teaching of the Lamb or of Christ), and their lives were consumed to death, Rv 12:11, are clearly called martyrs or witnesses of Jesus, Rv 17:6, and their testimony is praised. Reply: That is right, yet their confession, whether expressed orally or set down in writing, does not therefore constitute a new and subordinate principle of the truth. Otherwise the church would be infallible, providing the principle of the truth, as the papists say. The testimony of the faithful of the primitive church offers an example—not a principle—of believing.

XI. Observe: We do not deny the proposition: What the primitive church of the first five centuries from the birth of Christ taught, with unanimous consent proved from the most ancient ecumenical councils and the united testimonies of the ancient martyrs and fathers, it behooves us to confess today, and what it disapproved or rejected in line with Scripture it behooves us also to reject. But it does not follow from that proposition that that should in that sense be called a principle of believing; for what is not credible in itself, what needs the extension of ages, and what is not sufficient of itself, what is simply not necessary, what can be denied by some, etc. cannot properly be called a principle statement;

but all these things belong to this inferior principle, as they say, or sub-principle, as the Refutation of Crypto-Papism clearly teaches.

XII. Observe: The papists, especially the Jesuits and those who in part follow them, often have on [their] lips the rule of Vincent of Lérins, partly contemporaneous with Augustine (for the middle period of Vincent of Lérins as presbyter of a monastery falls into the last [period] of Augustine): "What he knew that not only one or two but all held, wrote, [and] taught equally with one and the same consensus, clearly commonly, [and] perseveringly, that, he also takes to mean, is to be believed without any doubt." But (1) Gerardus Joannes Vossius rightly observes that the whole *Commonitorium* of Vincent was written under the fictitious name of Peregrinus in hate and disparagement of St. Augustine; he uses the *Commonitorium* to attack his [Augustine's] teaching of predestination and of the dispensation of divine grace under the heading of profane words and novelties and falsely sets against him the letters of popes Celestine and Sixtus written to the Gauls; but he carps at his Massilian associates and fellow countrymen, Faustus, who was abbot in the monastery of Vincent of Lérins, and Cassianus, semi-Pelagians, without evidence. Hülsemann shows with eight reasons that Vincent of Lérins has no authority here and that his rule is foolish. And he teaches, among other things, that the older fathers not only never approved but also clearly rejected that rule of Vincent, "Whatever all writers together everywhere clearly, commonly, [and] consistently wrote, that only [and] alone is to be held for an article of faith and [for] the truth" etc., appealing to the clear and literal consensus that is among the prophets and apostles, as the Apology of the Augsburg Confession, Gerhard, and others have shown by introducing individual fathers.

XIII. Gregory of Valencia objects: "The harmonious belief of those whom, already from the time of the apostles, the church has in various ages venerated as fathers, originated from the Holy Spirit and [is] therefore infallible; it ought to be the more certain among us, the less it appears that it could have come about humanly that so many and such learned and most holy men, who lived at such varied times and places, agreed in the same belief." We reply (1) that the consensus of the fathers among themselves is here and there and often in harmony with divine truth—the reason for this agreement is not the consensus of those writers among themselves but with the whole communion of the faithful or without doubt such [who are] orthodox. The mark of infalliblity was added by Christ to that in which these agreed, not to that in which only the writers agree among themselves. (2) This begs the question, and that doubly: (a) Because it is supposed without good reason that there is to be found a common, clear, and constant consensus of individual and all writers on individual and all doctrines; (b) because it is supposed that the same ones who agree in some truths could not hold the same view in some other error. Indeed, distance as to places and ages does not help the matter.

Porism IV

And finally, no visions, apparitions, private revelations, and inner angelic messages are to be used in proving articles of faith.

The Point at Issue

The question is: Is the norm either of things to be believed or of things to be done to be drawn beyond or outside of Holy Scripture from special raptures and private revelations?

Exposition

I. Distinguish between visions and revelations given before the death of the apostles and [those] after their death and that reveal new articles of faith; the discussion here is not about the former but about the latter.

II. Distinguish between the unwritten Word, outward and inward. The former only the papists profess, the latter both papists and Enthusiasts as well as Socinians and some Calvinists [profess].

III. Observe: The Greeks call *enthousiasmos* or *enthousiasis* in general and formally afflatus and divine, and materially and objectively the power communicated by divine afflatus. "To be in ectasy" is to be held fast by the Spirit [that is] in God. Those who were held fast by the Spirit and were in ecstasy were also simply called *entheoi*, likewise *theophoroi, theophoroumenoi, pneumatophoroi*, likewise *theoleptoi*, etc., as is evident from Suidas.

IV. Distinguish between true divine afflatus and apparent [afflatus], which in turn is either fictitious or imaginary. We here speak of the latter kind of raptures, which ordinarily is usually called that, and thus by Enthusiasts we mean fanatic people who either invent or imagine afflatus, revelations, and inspirations of God and by calling either diabolical or melancholic or voluntary illusions and imaginations divine revelations deceive themselves and others.

V. Distinguish between God's power and His will. No one denies that God can give new revelations, but it is doubtful whether it be His will [to do so].

VI. Distinguish between the hidden and the revealed will of God. The latter is to be determined only from the written Word of God; of the former, which is hidden, nothing certain can be said.

Antithesis

I. Of various fanatics who hold: "The knowledge of God and of all doctrines that are to be believed is not to be sought from the written Word of God, but that of a higher wisdom than that contained in Holy Scriptures [is to be sought] from the special revelation made particularly to each individual and from the innate[170] light, from raptures, dreams, conversations with angels, from an internal word, from the inspiration (*Einsprechen*) of the heavenly Father, from internal knowledge of Christ, [who is] essentially united with them, [and] from the instruction of the Holy Spirit speaking and teaching internally." It is certain that very many fanatics, ancient and modern, were seized by such enthusiasm. With the ancients can be listed the Montanists, inasmuch as they professed visions of angels, Donatists, who [professed] dreams and apparitions, Adelphius and others, who [professed] ecstasies, previews of things to come, [and] an ocular vision of the most Holy Trinity. These are the words of the *Tripartite History:* "The heresy arose out of the disturbance of the Messalians, who are called *eucheetai,* that is, Orantes.[171] But they are called also by the other name of Enthusiasts, that is, men breathed upon and divines.[172] For they expect the operation of some daemon and regard this [operation] as the presence of the Holy Spirit. And those who participate in the whole weakness of this matter[173] turn away from manual labor as evil, give themselves over to idleness, and call the fantasies of [their] dreams prophecies. The leaders of this heresy were Dadoes and Sabbas, and Adelphius, Herman, and Symeones, and others." More recent Enthusiasts are those who, as our grandfathers and fathers remember, came forth out of the nether world under the detestable leadership and auspices of Thomas

Münzer, that seditious head of the Anabaptists in Thuringia, of Kasper von Schwenkfeld in Silesia, of Theophrastus Paracelsus in Switzerland, of Coppinus and Quintinus in Picardy, [and] Valentin Weigel in Meissen. All these contended that not only the written Word of God but also revelations, enthusiasms, dreams, and the direct voice of God were to be heard and that the government of the church was to be set up according to these things, as is clear partly from Johannes Sleidanus, from the infamous doctrine and practice of the Münster Anabaptists, and from the Colloquium of Antonius Corvinus and Johannes Kymäus, theologians of the Hessians, with John of Leiden, [who] lived at Bergen[174] in 1536, [and] partly from their writings. The Schwenkfelders indeed disparagingly called students of Holy Scripture wordists[175] and literalists, but made much of their own illuminations and revelations. Exactly the same[176] were the dreams of Theophrastus Paracelsus, of Valentin Weigel, and of Paul Nagel, and that kind of other fanatics. Hence the name Enthusiasts attaches to them, because of the enthusiasms and ecstasies and special raptures that they fancied and held that one must hold to them [the enthusiasms etc.] both in defining articles of faith and in establishing life practice. Add to these the Rosicrucian Brethren, the new prophets, John Warner, George Richard, [and] the Quakers, or Shakers, in England, who also dream up divine raptures and direct revelations. So also has Jean de Labadie publicly boasted of heavenly revelations, of conversations with the blessed saints, and of apparitions of the blessed Virgin Mary granted him while praying; and his followers assert that God often deals directly with the faithful without the Word and therefore they exhort that one should "take recourse to the inner revelations of the Spirit and give diligent attention to them" So also Schürmann[177] tries to prove that "besides Scripture" there are given also today "doctrinal prophecies" and inner revelations.

II. [Antithesis] of the papists. Dannhauer shows that

they admit among the principles of faith the revelations given to individuals, for example, Bridget, Catherine of Siena, etc. Cloppenburg shows that the papists deprecate the authority of Holy Scripture below the authority of the Spirit speaking inwardly in hearts, and thus they do the same as Enthusiasts and Schwenkfelders. Bellarmine proves the worship of relics from revelation. Valerian Magnus, a Capuchin, makes revelations and apparitions given outside of Scripture if not the only, certainly the main, foundation of the universal papistic faith.

III. Of the Socinians. Thus Faustus Socinus holds that Laelius Socinus (from this Laelius, the paternal uncle, and Faustus, [his] nephew, Socinus, natives of Siena, Etruscans, by nationality Italians, the name attached to that sect) by many prayers obtained from Christ Himself the interpretation of those words of Christ, Jn 8:58: "Before Abraham was[178] the father of many nations, I am the Light of the world,"[179] and that this [interpretation] was revealed to him by God Himself. Ostorodt demands direct revelations or special inner enlightenment for understanding the prophetic Scriptures and most of the Revelation of John.

IV. Of some Calvinists. Thus Andreas Karlstadt made much of private revelations and visions. Blessed Luther refuted him. Sleidanus says: "He of whom we spoke above, Karlstadt, disagreeing with Luther, left Wittenberg and was closely associated with the secret teachers that feigned visions and conversations with God, as we said before." And Huldreich Zwingli claims that it became known to him by special revelation, through the Spirit, that the word *est* [is] in the words of the Supper was put for *significat* [signifies]. Hence Dannhauer [says]: "If you look at the beginnings, Calvinism owes more than a little to the fanatic enthusiasm of Karlstadt and Zwingli, though it seems to have ceased later."

Confirmation of the Porism

We draw proofs of the orthodox view I. from the authority of Scripture, which calls us back from all other principles, from revelations and apparitions, "to the Law and to the Testimony," Is 8:20, to "Moses and the prophets," Lk 16:29. Christ commands: "Search the Scriptures," Jn 5:39. And Peter exhorts, 2 Ptr 1:19, that one should heed the prophetic Word "until the day dawn and the daystar arise in our hearts."

II. From the perfection of the Sacred Scriptures, which admits no additions of new revelations, Dt 12:32 and Rv 22:18. Every addition to Holy Scripture is forbidden under solemn anathema. Hence Tertullian [says]: "If it is not written, let him fear that 'Woe!' aimed at those who add and subtract." Gl 1:8 it is decreed that one is not even to believe an angel from heaven who preaches another gospel. 2 Ti 3:16–17 is taught the perfection and wholeness of Scripture, profitable for all uses, both theoretical and practical, and thus [is taught its] sufficiency to direct faith and life.

III. From the assurance of faith, which is to be sought only from the Holy Scriptures, Jn 20:31; 2 Ti 3:15. Thomas[180] says: "Our faith rests on the revelation given to the prophets and apostles who wrote the canonical books but not on revelations, if any, given to other teachers."

IV. Lack of a promise. Nowhere are direct revelations or visions promised to be expected in our times. In Lk 16:29 the condemned feaster is rebuked for requesting revelations of the dead for [his] brethren who survived [him] in [this] life.

V. From the diabolical fraud and deception in those revelations. For the devil seizes the opportunity to deceive people through this kind of apparitions under some divine pretext, as Gretser says.

VI. From the nature of those revelations, for they are obscure, dubious, uncertain, suspect, often absurd, deceptive, dangerous, unprofitable, unnecessary, contrary to the Word of God, subject to the hocus-pocus and mockeries of Satan, [and] subject to the judgment of others, 1 Co 14:29, 32, and therefore cannot be regarded as a principle of theology and of faith.

VII. The new prophets draw their prophecies not so much from special revelation as by a kind of plagiarism from Ezekiel, Daniel, and Revelation.

VIII. The angels whom the adversaries dream up either proclaim faithfully the same as that which is found in the Word or something other and different; if the latter, they are not to be heard, Gl 1:8; if the former, their revelation is unnecessary.

IX. By the revelations of the Enthusiasts (1) the order of the ministry, or the order among teachers and learners divinely established in the church, is overturned; (2) the ranks set up in the Christian church are mixed up; (3) the certainty of faith is destroyed; (4) the door is opened to some impersonators [and] imposters and their heresies and errors. Therefore [the revelations of the Enthusiasts] cannot be a rule of things to be believed or done.

Hülsemann well says: "It is not only not safe but also not licit to desire angelic revelations; I would say [this] not [only] about matters of faith but also about the extrinsic accidents of the ecclesiastical, political, or economic estate." The same: "Today no revelation occurs by direct infusion—by God or angels, without human ministry—of things to be believed, in the mind of those who are to be saved. Heb 1:2–3: In time past God indeed spoke to people in many ways—by visions, by dreams, [and] by prophecies, but finally through [His] Son. 1 Co 13:8: For prophecies also will come to an end, and tongues will cease, and direct knowledge will stop after the Gospel of the Gentiles has become known every-where[181] [Mt 24:14]."

Refutation

I. The adversaries object: Scripture is to be heard because it is inspired by God, 2 Ti 3:16, and thus both prophecies and enthusiasms [are to be heard] for the same reason, for they are divinely inspired dictamen, because every word of the true God[182] is to be heard. We reply: We grant that [Scripture] is to be heard because it is divinely inspired, but we deny that the enthusiasms that those fanatic people boast of are such. The contrary is clear from what follows, for those enthusiasms and the teachings spread through them assail the teaching of the Holy Spirit and subvert it, as is clear from a comparison of the first Münster Anabaptism[183] and the lawlessness and disorders introduced thereby in the civil government, and likewise from the ravings of the Schwenkfelders and Weigelians. But the Holy Spirit is not yes and no, 2 Co 1:19, nor [is] the Spirit either the author or the supporter of disturbances, uprisings, and crimes. (2) Distinguish between the true voice of God and a false [voice], [between] the authentic [voice] and a putative and imaginary [voice]. The former, which does not speak today except in Holy Scripture, is to be heeded, not the latter.

II. They object that Scripture alone is to be heard when special inspirations and revelations are not given, not where they are given. We reply: This presupposes that Scripture is not to be heard in the church always and continually. But since Scripture is the voice of God, as the adversaries also admit, and it [is] given to this end, that by it the man of God might be made perfect, surely it is continually and always to be heard. (2) One errs in the false supposition that special inspirations and revelations are given with regard to the things that are to be believed or done outside of Scripture. (3) Those inspirations and revelations are either like Scripture and the truth revealed in it, or not. If they are like it, they are not outside of Scripture, but as they are subjectively in the mind, so are they objectively in Scripture. If they are not like it, they cannot be divine inspirations, for the revelations of God can also not be contrary to themselves.

III. They object that "testimony" in Is 8:20 is a generic word and can be understood either of written testimony or testimony communicated by revelation from heaven [and] that besides the writings of Moses and some prophets other heavenly inspirations and revelations were recognized. We reply: (1) We grant that "testimony" is a generic word and can be understood also of testimony from heaven by revelation communicated to prophets in the Old Testament. But we deny that such testimony is [that] of the enthusiasts, since the former agrees with the Law, that is, Holy Scripture, in fact it is the same as it, [but] the latter by no means. (2) In the oracle of Isaiah, what is first called Law, then Testimony, is finally called Word; and that Word, which is now for enlightenment and the public good explained as the regular and unquestioned norm of things to be said, is the written Word of God. (3) One errs in the proof of equals and of the consequence.[184] Heavenly inspirations and revelations had a [valid] place in the Old Testament. Ergo also today. Then it was the time of prophecies, but Christ teaches, Mt 11:13, that that age lasted only until John.

IV. They object that a search of the Scriptures is commended in Jn 5:39, but not only or exclusively. Otherwise also later writings of the New Testament, not yet recorded at the time of Christ, when this was said, should be excluded. We reply: (1) Since the Lord in Jn 5:39 referred the Jews to the Scriptures and said that they testify of Him, they either sufficiently testify of Christ or they do not. If the former, there is no need of new revelations; if the latter, they are imperfect and Christ did not sufficiently show them the way to know Him. (2) What need is there of other revelations if we can have eternal life from the Scriptures? (3) One errs in the proof of equals. For the nature of superadded Scriptures and their divine inspirations through apostles is one thing, [but] the nature of the inspirations of the fanatics, thrust forward without basis as divinely inspired, is another. For the former are also Scriptures to be searched, which testify of Christ, and [are] indeed revelations divinely inspired and credible in themselves, but the fanatic [revelations] not likewise.

V. They object that perforce the passage in Lk 16:29 can be turned around; for if the prophets [are] to be heard, also the enthusiasms, that is divine revelations are to be heard. We reply: (1) It does not follow [to say]: The prophets are to be heard, ergo the prophets that appeared after those times [are to be heard]. The command is that the prophets are to be heard who were extant already at that time and whom the brothers of the epicure could consult. (2) By the designation "the prophets" Christ did not mean the prophets considered personally, but practically, really, that is, the writings of the prophets; this is clear from the added name of Moses, because it is certain that, with equal reason,[185] it is to be understood not of the person but of the writings of Moses; for Moses could no longer be heard, having died long before. (3) Perforce this very thing can be turned around: As God did not want Lazarus to be heard as a prophet, but the writings of Moses and the prophets, so today He also does not want the fanatic inspirations outside of Scripture to be heard.

VI. They object that the passage in 2 Ptr 1:19 can also be turned around: For since one is to heed the prophetic Word, one is also to heed the enthusiasms, which are a prophetic word. In fact, the daystar truly arises in hearts when inner revelations occur to the servants or sons of God. We reply: (1) The prophetic Word, of which Peter speaks there, is not the word taken formally, but materially, not verbally but practically, namely related in the writings of the prophets. And "prophetic Word" here is the same as what Peter calls "prophecy of Scripture" in verse 20. The same is clear from the predicate adjective, for one could not heed the oral word of the ancient prophecies, since they had long ago already ceased among the living, and thus one could not heed them in any other way than insofar as one heeded the prophecy of Scripture, that is, the written prophecy. (2) [This] does not follow: One must heed the prophetic Word divinely inspired and recorded in writings by divine impulse; therefore one must heed the fanatic inspirations. In fact, since one should heed the prophetic Word, one should not heed that kind of inspirations, since the prophetic Word calls us back to the Law and the Testimony, Is 8:20. (3) It begs the question [to say] that the daystar then arises in hearts when that kind of fanatic inspirations are extolled; in fact, the day and the daystar then arises, when the sons of God are translated into the heavenly fatherland, which needs no sun, and when God will fully illumine their heart, Rv 22:5.

VII. They object that in Dt 5:32 and 12:32 additions are not absolutely forbidden by God, thus divinely inspired prophecies [are] not [forbidden]. I reply: I agree, but I deny that [those] of the fanatics are divinely inspired prophecies. And since those ravings are not prophetic inspirations of God, they should therefore not be received as such.

VIII. They object that in Gl 1:8 it is only forbidden that those who preach another gospel be heard, and they are those who overturn the doctrine of the Gospel; but, to be exact, the true sense of the Gospel and its spiritual meaning is opened by enthusiasms. Reply: (1) Since in Gl 1:8 those who preach another gospel are prohibited, the fanatics mentioned above are prohibited; they teach another gospel regarding the person of Christ, regarding the origin of the human nature of Christ, regarding His offices and benefits, [and] regarding the Sacraments instituted by Him—plainly contrary to the Gospel preached by Paul to the Galatians. (2) It is false that the true sense of the Gospel and its spiritual meaning are opened by enthusiasms; in fact, it is, rather, perverted and overturned, and that spiritual meaning of the fanatics destroys the true doctrine taught in the Scriptures. (3) The one spiritual meaning is innate [in] Scripture and drawn out of it, the other [is] privately introduced [and] stuffed into Scripture. The former we receive; the latter we reject.

IX. They object that the prohibition of addition in Rv 22:18 refers only to the Book of Revelation and that by that sanction are forbidden not so much prophetic impulses and raptures as others ways of setting forth Scripture or the will of God. I reply: (1) That closing prohibition indeed refers directly to the Book of Revelation, but I deny that it does not want those words by equivalence in meaning to be a sign and end-marker of divinely inspired revelations. (2) One thing is [that] of the impulses and raptures of the fanatics, another is [that] of the proper ways of setting forth the will of God or Scripture. And the conclusion is added, that that way, through enthusiastic raptures, is the proper one. However, only that exposition is to be received which interprets Scripture from Scripture and according to the analogy of faith.

Sources of Rebuttals

I. Many things have been truly predicted by them in a prophetic spirit that the story of our times has verified. Reply: (1) That begs the question, and revelations of future events and their predictions are boasted of, not proved. (2) The false hypothesis is posited that all predictions of future things are prophetic, or divinely inspired. But there are also many devil-inspired, many natural, many conjectural, many casual, many ambiguous and purely theatrical; most such among the Gentiles issue from various oracles and prophets of the devil, who would also have to be venerated among the true prophets, if an argument is to be drawn from the prediction of some future things.

II. They object that a very sorry state of the church is represented by the lack of prophets, Ps 74:9. Reply: (1) The nature of the Old Testament is one, that of the New [is] another. The psalmist speaks of the former, not of the latter. The mission of the prophets belonged to the Old Testament, not to the New. (2) The statement there is about the lack not only of prophets but also of signs of the presence of God, of the ark, Urim and Thummim, sacrifices, etc., but our status is different: We have the prophets, the prophecy of Scripture, to which we do well to give heed; [and] we have the Sacraments, etc., and thus there is no need of extraordinary revelations to proclaim to us the presence of God.

III. Distinguish between revelations that pertain to or attack an article of faith and [those] that concern the state of the church or the state, social life, and future events. We reject the former. But some hold that the latter are not indeed to be urged with any necessity of believing and yet are not to be rejected rashly. Balduin says: "We do not doubt that God still at times reveals to some people future things that pertain to the state of the church and of the state, to be announced for the benefit of people."

IV. Distinguish between true Samuel and Samuel impersonated, or his ghost. Not the former but the latter appeared to Saul, 1 Sm 28. For the circumstances of the text show, and Thomas[186] himself, Juan de Torquemada, Cajetan, and others also acknowledge that the hocus-pocus was of Satan; and thus that refutes rather than supports revelations.

V. Distinguish between anointing by enthusiasm and anointing obtained, or to be obtained, by the Word of God, by which the anointing of the Holy Spirit itself is communicated to us. 1 Jn 2:27 speaks not of the former, but of the latter. "The Word of God is spirit and life,"

Jn 6:63. The Holy Spirit is communicated by it, not by enthusiasm, Gl 3:2. That anointing is the Holy Spirit, the principle cause of faith; He instructs us, not directly, but by means of the Word, 1 Jn 2:14; 1 Th 2:13; Ro 10:17. This is the meaning of the words of the apostle: "You have been so knowledgeably and faithfully instructed by the apostles regarding Christ and the rest of the articles of faith, by the operation of the Holy Spirit, that you need no other misleading teachers" (for he speaks of them in the immediately preceding verse, 1 Jn 2:26), "who teach you something else." And this [applies] to the revelations and phantasms of the fanatics.

VI. They counter with Jl 2:28: "I will pour out of My Spirit upon all flesh, and your sons and your daughters will prophecy; your old men will dream dreams and your young men will see visions." Therefore, either that prophecy is false, or must leave room for prophecies, visions, dreams and extraordinary operations of the Spirit of God. Reply: That speaks of the outpouring of the Holy Spirit on the apostles, [as] Peter testifies in Acts 2:16–17, and therefore it is falsely applied to others. (2) In this passage dreams and visions denote a more abundant knowledge of God, however perceived from outward proclamation and drawn from the Scripture, in the usual manner by prophets, who usually describe the state of the Old Testament sometimes in figurative words or words that suit the Old Testament state. And therefore the prophet speaks of the excellence and prerogative of the gifts of God to be given under the economy of the New Testament, both [1] intensively, because God would in it pour out His light and grace, Jl 2:28–29, and thus would grant it in a large measure and greater variety of gifts than in the Old, Jl 2:29, and [2] extensively, because God would bestow that favor on many, without distinction of condition, sex, or age. Therefore, when the adversaries insist that those prophetic words are to be understood literally regarding visions and dreams, and not in the sense now set forth by us, regarding the abundant light and knowledge of God to be poured out in the New Testament on all kinds [of people], we reply: Those [words] are not to be taken literally, and the universal joint predicate, "all flesh," is to be understood in accordance with the mind of the prophet and the style of Scripture. Even if this is to be understood absolutely of all, also literally handmaidens and servants, yet those new prophets will have nothing singular more than their hearers.

VII. Observe Jer 31:33: "I will put My law into their inner parts and write it on their hearts." The statement is not of direct inspiration of the Word, but of the proclamation of the Gospel (which is the law of faith, Ro 3:27; the law of the Spirit of life in Christ Jesus, Ro 8:2), as is clear from Heb 8:10. And it speaks of the Law to be written in hearts, not by direct revelation, but by means of the written and proclaimed Word of God, and a difference between Law and Gospel is intimated. The Law written on tables of stone, not indeed by God's intention yet nevertheless by its operation restrains only the outward conduct of people, Ro 7:8–9, but neither penetrates to the heart nor cleanses conscience itself, Heb 9:13–14. But the Gospel penetrates hearts and is impressed on conscience itself, 2 Co 3:3; Ro 1:16; Heb 4:12. But it is one thing to penetrate hearts and another to be inspired or inscribed in hearts. Briefly: God does not speak of inscription that is done enthusiastically and by bare inspiration, but by hearing, by the Word heard or read. Nor does the phrase "to be written in the heart" imply an inner afflatus, by any kind of impression, whether made by nature, Ro 2:14, or by teaching, 2 Co 3:2; Pr 3:3.

VIII. Observe 1 Co 14:30: "If [something] be revealed to another sitting by, let the first be silent." The apostle there speaks of New Testament prophets, whose call was proper and who had an extraordinary gift. But here the question is about the kind of prophets who for the most part can show by any divine testimony neither a proper call nor an extraordinary gift or endowment. And yet they want and command that their fabrications be received without further investigation. It therefore in no way follows from this statement of the apostle that in the Christian church there will be some to whom direct revelations about matters of faith and life occur. For the gift of which the apostle there speaks by no means needs to be perpetual and regular in the church of Christ, but temporary, until the fullnes of the unbelieving Gentile will have come into the faith of Christ, as the apostle adds, 1 Co 14:21–22.[187]

IX. They object that God made prophets in the New Testament, 1 Co 12:28; Eph 4:11 and that there is said to be revealed to these prophets by the Spirit that which in other ages did not become known to the sons of men; therefore the prophecies of such should not be despised, Eph 3:5. Reply: (1) The ranks of the ordinary and [those] of the extraordinary ministry are confused, [as are] the fixed ranks of the church to be established with the fixed ranks of the established church. The ranks of the former kind were the prophets and apostles, [those] of the latter [kind], pastors and teachers. And as there were extraordinary ministers in the primitive church, so also were there in it extraordinary gifts, of prophecy, powers, healings, and the gift of tongues, etc., so that, with those props in place, the vault or arch of the Christian church might well come together; this done, those props were removed. (2) If by virtue of this arrangement prophets are given today, by the same line of thought apostles will also be given. (3) There is moreover hidden here a homonym in the word "prophets," which [a] sometimes properly means either prophets and foretellers of future things by divine revelation or those who, by direct gifts, have the singular and extraordinary ability to explain Scripture, 1 Co 12:29–30, [b] sometimes wrongly those who do not have divine inspirations and the gift of interpretation, but liars and those who by new and false teachings delude others. The former interpret Scripture properly and truly; the latter do not interpret but either overturn or pervert. Paul speaks of the former kind of prophets, not of the latter kind of prophets. (4) In Eph 3:5 Paul speaks of the same prophets as are spoken of by the same term in 1 Co 12:28; Eph 4:11. For they are assigned to the same order with the apostles, and they are meant to whom the mystery of Christ was already revealed; such are spoken of Acts 11:27-28; 13:1; 15:32; Ro 12:6. And such are called prophets (1) because, like the ancient prophets, they were raised not by indirect call through people, but by a direct [call] from God through His Spirit; (2) because, like the [ancient] prophets, they had obtained knowledge of divine things not by human effort but by divine revelation; (3) because, like the ancient prophets, they had the gift of interpreting the Word of God and of applying it to the present practices of the church; (4) because, like the ancient prophets, some revelations of future things sometimes occurred to them. Yet those prophets were inferior to the apostles; hence ["prophets"] is always put after them [the apostles], 1 Co 12:28; Eph 3:5; 4:11.

X. They object: Prophecy, even indeed given to some, not all, is clearly reckoned among the gifts of the Spirit, 1 Co 12:10, equally with the word of wisdom, faith, discerning of spirits, and others. And those are perpetual in the church; ergo also this. Reply: (1) We grant that prophecy was a gift of the Spirit such as occurred to prophets, of whom we have already spoken, and that it did not occur to all but only to some. But we deny that God wanted those gifts to be perpetual in the church. (2) Prophecy ought to be perpetual, namely partly objectively, prophecy of the Scripture, partly subjectively, the gift of interpreting it. Therefore it does not follow [to say that] prophecy ought to be perpetual in church, ergo the inspirations and revelations of which the fanatics boast are such prophecy. (3) The nature of ordinary gifts is one thing; another thing [is the nature] of extraordinary [gifts], which the apostle mentions there, such as were working of miracles, kinds of tongues, and prophecy; their nature is one thing, [but the nature] of the word of wisdom and of faith [is] another, for these are perpetually necessary, [but] those not likewise.

XI. They object: The Spirit bears witness on earth, 1 Jn 5:8; every spirit that confesses that Jesus Christ has come into the flesh is of God, 1 Jn 4:2. Reply: (1) One errs in the misinterpretation of the passage and in the homonym in the word "Spirit." The line of thought is also drawn affirmatively from the general to the particular: The Spirit is said to testify on earth; ergo the Spirit of the Enthusiasts. But *pneuma* there is the Word of the Spirit, the ministry of the Spirit, 2 Co 3:8, which bears witness on earth together with the two New Testament sacraments, the water of regeneration and the blood of cleansing from sins. (2) On the passage in 1 Jn 4:2 we reply: The Spirit of the Enthusiasts does not acknowledge that Jesus Christ has come into flesh like ours, and it does not hold fast the salutary doctrine of the revelation of Christ in the flesh and its manner, purpose, efficacy, and fruit, and thus [that Spirit] is not of God.

XII. They object: The apostle Paul clearly says, 1 Th 5:19–20: "The Spirit is not to be quenched, nor are prophecies to be regarded as nothing." Reply: By "Spirit" there is not to be understood here a fanatic Spirit, but the impulses of the Holy Spirit kindled in the hearts of the faithful, which [impulses] (like the sacred fire of old) are always to be fanned, lest they be extinguished, and they ought to be rekindled, 2 Ti 1:6. Thus by prophecies are not to be understood enthusiasms, but either objectively the prophetic Scriptures, or instrumentally their explanation and application, whether by special gift (of which kind of prophecy the statement in 1 Co 12 and 14 deals) or by common and ordinary gift.

Notes

1. *absolvitur.*
2. *principium.*
3. *principiatum.*
4. *eius.* Objective genitive.
5. *sermo Dei.*
6. *Dei loquium.*
7. *descendunt.*
8. *sermo de Deo.*
9. *confiteri.*
10. *sermo.*
11. *astrorum sermo.*
12. *sermo.*
13. *objective.*
14. *fertur.*
15. Thomas Aquinas.
16. *materia.*
17. *finis.*
18. *principalis.*
19. *objectum.*
20. *sermo.*
21. *adaequatum.*
22. *inadaequatum.*
23. *ordinatur.*
24. *sermo.*
25. John of Damascus.
26. *absolute.*
27. *aequivocatio.*
28. *opinabilis.*
29. *ex propriis.*
30. *principium.*
31. This is not against Jews as a racial group but only against error in religion. Cf. the explanation of Thesis VIII: "The church . . . is gathered from Gentiles and Jews. . . . God would have . . . Jews . . . saved."
32. *q. d. = quasi dicat.*
33. *corpus doctrinae.*
34. or repeated; *secundaria.* Hence "repetition" or "instruction by repetition."
35. *prona.*
36. *proxima.*
37. Old name of Paris.
38. *B. = Beatus;* entered into heaven; euphemism for "dead."
39. Reading *infinite* instead of *infinita;* or "as endless."
40. *scripturaria* = according to the writing.
41. *rara.*
42. Greek *proskairos,* "for the time."
43. *Batavi.*
44. See Thesis II.
45. Shaped after a model.
46. *pro modo ipsorum.*
47. *non est univoci in suo univocata, sed analogi in sua analogata.*
48. *habitus.* Cf. F. Pieper, *Christian Dogmatics,* I, 44.
49. *habitualis.*
50. Johann Crell.
51. *anima.*
52. Johann Heinrich Alsted.
53. *saltem.*
54. Hieronymus Zanchi.
55. David Pareus.
56. Literally "and": *alioque.*
57. Markus Friedrich Wendelin.
58. *habitualiter.*
59. *habitualis.*
60. Jesper Rasmussen Brochmand.
61. *habitualis.*
62. *saltem.*
63. *habitualis.*

64. *respectu sui.*
65. *non est nobis sermo.*
66. Thomas Aquinas
67. *Magistra Ecclesia.*
68. The Reims-Douay Version: "on whom"; the 1941 translation of The Confraternity of Christian Doctrine: "Into these things."
69. *prospiciunt.*
70. *patriae.*
71. *principium.*
72. *habitualis.*
73. *per gratiam creationis.*
74. *habitus.*
75. *actualis.*
76. *materia in qua.*
77. *actu.*
78. *principium.*
79. *materia circa quam.*
80. Peter the Lombard.
81. *praeditus.*
82. *individua.*
83. *ad.*
84. *vetustas.*
85. Greek: *prophorikos.*
86. *distinctis vicibus.*
87. *habitualis.*
88. *actu.*
89. *proficiuntur.*
90. *theologia naturalis.*
91. *spectata.*
92. *habitualis.*
93. Or: natural knowledge of God.
94. *sensus.*
95. *compositio.*
96. *ordinatio.*
97. *species.*
98. *altera vita.*
99. Daniel Heinsius.
100. Giovanni Stefano Menochio.
101. Jacob Tirinus.
102. *objecti vice.*
103. Heb 5:13.
104. *acroamatica.*
105. Heb 5:14.
106. *auditores.*
107. Singular subject, plural verb in the Latin.
108. *Objectum . . . sunt.*
109. *imperfectis.*
110. or casuistic; Latin *casualis.*
111. *commentariis conficiendis.*
112. *compater.*
113. *practicarum.*
114. *Subjectum . . . sunt.*
115. Konrad Horn(eius).
116. *animus.*
117. *relate.*
118. *acceptio.*
119. *habitus.*
120. Hilary of Poitiers.
121. Also spelled Baez and Baeza; b. Lisbon, Port.; active in Coimbra; court preacher of the king in Spain; d. 1638.
122. *causa media.*
123. Johann Friedrich König.
124. *religio.*
125. *conservarunt.*
126. *qua.*
127. *beabilis.*
128. or casuistic; Latin *casualis.*
129. *posita.*
130. *ponitur.*
131. *remotio.*
132. *positio.*
133. That is, the order is established.
134. *Fontes solutionum.*
135. That is, the aptitude to draw conclusions.
136. *proprius.*
137. Without the proclamation of the Word.
138. Without the ministry of people who are theologians.
139. *habitualiter.*
140. *inventio.*
141. *aeque principaliter eam respicit.*
142. cf. Ja 1:17.
143. *citra relationem.*
144. *Thomas Argentinensis.*
145. Jean Capreolus (ca. 1380–1444).
146. *comparatum.*
147. Petrus Aureolus (d. 1321).
148. Balthasar Meisner.
149. The Latin text has II.
150. *altera vita.*

151. *finis.*
152. Christoph Gill (Aegidius); prof. theol. Coimbra and Evora, Port.; d. 1608.
153. *religati.*
154. *religamus.*
155. *in specie.*
156. *ultro liquet.*
157. *adhuc sub judice lis sit.*
158. Or: this. Latin *huic.* Schonfield: this. Beck: All the prophets declare that through His name . . . .
159. Should this read "Socinians"?
160. As "Gospel" in the wide sense, e. g. Mk 16:15, includes the Law.
161. The Latin has a play on words: *verbis potius, quam verberibus.*
162. *cudit.*
163. H. Schmid, *Doctrinal Theology of the Evangelical Lutheran Church,* p. 31: "means of becoming acquainted with Theology." Lat.: *adminicula Theologiae acquirendae.*
164. Balthasar Mentzer the Elder (1565–1627).
165. *minime corruptus*
166. *forum.*

167. Ger.: *vielgemelter*
168. *tesseralis.*
169. *succus et sanguis.*
170. *congenita.*
171. Literally "those who pray."
172. Or: divinely inspired. Latin: *divini.*
173. Pieper-Engelder, *Christian Dogmatics,* I, 209: Those who have given themselves over entirely to this disease.
174. *Bevergae.*
175. *Vocalistas.*
176. *Gemina.*
177. Anna Maria von Schürmann.
178. *fiat.* In Jn 8:58 the word is *fieret.*
179. Cf. Jn 8:12; 9:5.
180. Thomas Aquinas.
181. *postquam Evangelium ubique gentium innotuit.*
182. Or: of the truth of God. Latin: *veri Dei.*
183. *Anabaptismi primi Munzeriani.*
184. *Peccatur elencho parium et consequentiae.* That is, it is a *non sequitur.*
185. *pari ratione.*
186. Thomas Aquinas.
187. Cf. Ro 11:25.